Bigger Faster Stronger

SECOND EDITION

Greg Shepard, EdD

Human Kinetics

Library of Congress Cataloging-in-Publication Data

Shepard, Greg, 1942-
 Bigger, faster, stronger / Greg Shepard. -- 2nd ed.
   p. cm.
 Includes bibliographical references and index.
 ISBN-13: 978-0-7360-7963-1 (soft cover)
 ISBN-10: 0-7360-7963-7 (soft cover)
 1. High school athletes--Training of. 2. School sports. 3. Physical education and training--Study and teaching (Secondary) I. Title.
 GV346.S55 2009
 613.7'11--dc22

                           2008054277

ISBN-10: 0-7360-7963-7 (print)   ISBN-10: 0-7360-8207-7 (Adobe PDF)
ISBN-13: 978-0-7360-7963-1 (print)   ISBN-13: 978-0-7360-8207-5 (Adobe PDF)

Copyright © 2009 by Bigger Faster Stronger
Copyright © 2004 by Greg Shepard

All rights reserved. Except for use in a review, the reproduction or utilization of this work in any form or by any electronic, mechanical, or other means, now known or hereafter invented, including xerography, photocopying, and recording, and in any information storage and retrieval system, is forbidden without the written permission of the publisher.

Notice: Permission to reproduce the following material is granted to instructors and agencies who have purchased *Bigger Faster Stronger:* figure 17.5. The reproduction of other parts of this book is expressly forbidden by the above copyright notice. Persons or agencies who have not purchased *Bigger Faster Stronger* may not reproduce any material.

Acquisitions Editors: Jessica Gosney and Laurel Plotzke; **Developmental Editor:** Kevin Matz; **Assistant Editor:** Elizabeth Watson; **Copyeditor:** Alisha Jeddeloh; **Proofreader:** Kathy Bennett; **Indexer:** Nan N. Badgett; **Graphic Designer:** Nancy Rasmus; **Graphic Artist:** Tara Welsch; **Cover Designer:** Keith Blomberg; **Photographs (cover):** © Bigger Faster Stronger™ except bottom middle © Averin Collier, Democrat and Chronicle; **Photographs (interior):** © Bigger Faster Stronger™ unless otherwise noted; **Photo Production Manager:** Jason Allen; **Art Manager:** Kelly Hendren; **Associate Art Manager:** Alan L. Wilborn; **Illustrations:** © Bigger Faster Stronger™; **Printer:** United Graphics

Human Kinetics books are available at special discounts for bulk purchase. Special editions or book excerpts can also be created to specification. For details, contact the Special Sales Manager at Human Kinetics.

Printed in the United States of America   10 9

The paper in this book is certified under a sustainable forestry program.

Human Kinetics
Web site: www.HumanKinetics.com

United States: Human Kinetics, P.O. Box 5076, Champaign, IL 61825-5076
800-747-4457
email: humank@hkusa.com

Canada: Human Kinetics, 475 Devonshire Road Unit 100, Windsor, ON N8Y 2L5
800-465-7301 (in Canada only)
email: info@hkcanada.com

Europe: Human Kinetics, 107 Bradford Road, Stanningley, Leeds LS28 6AT, United Kingdom
+44 (0) 113 255 5665
email: hk@hkeurope.com

Australia: Human Kinetics, 57A Price Avenue, Lower Mitcham, South Australia 5062
08 8372 0999
e-mail: info@hkaustralia.com

New Zealand: Human Kinetics, P.O. Box 80, Torrens Park, South Australia 5062
0800 222 062
e-mail: info@hknewzealand.com

James R. Benson

Bigger
Faster
Stronger

SECOND EDITION

CONTENTS

Acknowledgments vi
Introduction vii

Part I The Total Program

1 Unified Approach to Training 3
2 BFS Rotational Set-Rep System 11
3 BFS In-Season Training 25
4 BFS Readiness Program 35

Part II Strength Exercises

5 Six Absolutes of Perfect Technique 49
6 Parallel Squat and Squat Variations 63
7 Power Clean and Quick Lifts 81
8 Hex-Bar Deadlift and Deadlift Variations 93
9 Bench Press and Bench Press Variations 103
10 Sport-Specific Auxiliary Lifts 113

Part III Speed, Agility, and Flexibility

11	Agility and the BFS Dot Drill	133
12	Five-Phase Plyometric Program	139
13	Speed Training	147
14	BFS 1-2-3-4 Flexibility Program	155

Part IV Program Administration

15	Organization and Weight Room Design	167
16	Safety and Liability	177
17	BFS Nutritional Plan	185
18	Be an Eleven	193
19	Why Steroids Don't Work	201

Appendix	207
Index	221
About the Author	227

ACKNOWLEDGMENTS

I would like to acknowledge those individuals who have helped throughout the years in developing my knowledge of strength and conditioning: Dr. Phil Allsen, Coach Gerald Crittenden, Coach Al Decoria, George Frenn, Dr. Lavon Johnson, Coach Herb Langeman, Dr. Ed Reuter, Coach Vert Shell, Dr. L. Jay Silvester, and Don Tollefson.

Thanks also to our Bigger Faster Stronger (BFS) clinicians: Evan Ayers, Rick Bojak, Bob Bozied, Jim Brown, P.J. Brown, Brynn Cogdill, Ray Cosenza, Bob Doyle, Dennis Dunn, Mandy Eddy, Doug Ekmark, Roger Freeborn, Mike Glennie, Eric Gobble, Nick Goshe, Peter Gregg, Patti Hagemeyer, John Halland, Doug Holland, Doug Kaufusi, Erich Mach, Steve Price, Jeff Scurran, Jeff Sellers, Tom Sullivan, Rick Tomberlin, Len Walencikowski, Randy Walker, and Tom Wilson.

Special thanks to my BFS partners: BFS president Bob Rowbotham and BFS vice president John Rowbotham, BFS editor-in-chief Kim Goss, and the thousands of coaches and athletes who have participated in the BFS program and clinics. And special thanks to my wife, Diana Shepard, for proofreading this book.

INTRODUCTION

You can't argue with success. More than 9,000 high schools have implemented the Bigger Faster Stronger (BFS) program since 1976, and of these schools, more than 400 have won state championships in football after attending BFS clinics. Many college teams and high-profile professional athletes are making dramatic improvements with BFS, and each year our clinicians schedule more than 400 seminars.

The popularity of the BFS program has reached such a level that in one independent survey through the University of Minnesota, 40 percent of the high school football coaches polled said they use BFS as their primary source of strength and conditioning information, and more than 250,000 students have gone through a BFS clinic. What this means is that BFS is not one of those workouts that is here today, gone tomorrow; it is a popular and effective training method with a 33-year history of success.

What is not widely known is how the BFS program developed from events that are a vital component of the achievements of BFS today. As I think about the origins of today's BFS, I can point to three primary sources. First, there's George Frenn, who personifies the throwers in track and field in the late 1960s who achieved remarkable results on the field and in the weight room. Second, there are the high school and college athletes I coached from the mid-1960s to the late 1970s, the very first BFS athletes. Finally, there's the late Stefan Fernholm, an elite discus thrower. Stefan shared many remarkable training methods, especially in the area of proper technique, from the Eastern Bloc nations in the 1980s. All these athletes provided the practical experience to refine the BFS system so it could be easily taught and implemented in the United States.

GEORGE FRENN'S SECRET

By the late 1960s, I had already been a high school football coach and a strength coach at the University of Oregon and Oregon State, and before that I had trained with the San Diego Chargers, who at that time were at the forefront of weight training for pro football. I had won many powerlifting competitions, including the national collegiate championships, and I was a member of an Olympic weightlifting team in Salzburg, Austria. I had also paid my dues academically, eventually earning a doctorate in physical education. So as far as training knowledge and experience go, I didn't exactly just fall off the turnip truck. But, when I saw George Frenn train, I knew I still had a great deal to learn.

One of the best hammer throwers in the country, George had a best competitive squat of 843 pounds (382 kilograms), long before the days of super suits and other supportive equipment. He was so far ahead of everyone else that it was obvious there was something different about his training. I wanted to know his secrets! So, in the late 1960s, I spent my summers in the Los Angeles area to be near George and pick his brain.

Also joining George were many other elite throwers who came from all over the country to live in the Los Angeles area, where they could throw all year round with many of the best athletes in the world. As a football coach, I looked at these guys and was amazed at their conditioning. There were at least 30 of them, and they weighed an average of 270 pounds (123 kilograms) and ran 4.6 to 4.7 seconds in the 40-yard (37-meter) dash. They were far bigger, faster, and stronger than the professional football players of that era, and I wanted those types of athletes on my football team.

George was the master, along with Jon Cole, a discus thrower who squatted 905 pounds (411 kilograms) and deadlifted 880 pounds (399 kilograms) in powerlifting competitions. Jon also entered a few Olympic lifting meets and, with best lifts of 430 pounds (195 kilograms) in the standing Olympic press, 340 pounds (154 kilograms) in the snatch, and 430 pounds (195 kilograms) in the clean and jerk, he came close to making the U.S. Olympic team in weightlifting. Everybody learned from Jon and George. Athletes from the Soviet Union were even in awe of these two, and their coaches and athletes came over to the United States to observe and learn. We were the dominant force in the world at that time in the throwing events, and everybody wanted our secret.

What was the secret? It was simple, but it was quite radical at the time: Stretch, lift hard with free weights, vary workouts, and concentrate on the big multijoint lifts that develop the legs and hips. You've got to do that, plus add sprinting and jump training.

This means that all athletes, regardless of their sport, should focus their strength training on the squat and the power clean. These lifts may be augmented by doing a few, but only a few, auxiliary lifts, and the lifting and stretching should be complemented with speed and plyometric jump drills. They're simple ideas, but they're the best.

FIRST BFS ATHLETES

The next contribution to BFS came when I took what I learned from George back to my high school. In 1970 I was a coach at Sehome High School in Bellingham, Washington. Sehome's enrollment of 1,400 nudged us into being considered a big school, but it was among the smallest in its classification. Despite our size, we won the unofficial state championship against a school with almost twice our enrollment. Our athletes were simply too good—the only thing the opposing team could produce in that championship game was minus 77 yards (70 meters)! I also coached boys track, and 11 of our athletes could throw the discus between 140 and 180 feet (43 and 55 meters). If you couldn't throw 155 feet (47 meters), you were on the junior varsity team; to this day I don't believe any high school has ever been able to say that. And we had bunches of kids who could bench 300 pounds (136 kilograms), squat 400 pounds (181 kilograms), and power clean 250 pounds (113 kilograms)—lifts that college athletes would be proud of.

My next challenge was as head football coach at a high school in Idaho. I inherited a team that was 0–6 and had lost homecoming 72–0; the kids were so dispirited that they just quit, forfeiting their last three games. We trained hard, and the following year our team won the county championships and scored a fantastic 29–16 victory over the team that had beat us 72–0. And this was despite the fact that the opposing team had a school enrollment of 1,600 kids to our 850! Then I took over the Granger High School football team in Salt Lake City, a team that had won only two games in four years, and we achieved what is still considered the most dramatic turnaround in the history of Utah. This got everyone's attention.

Coaches were asking me, "How can you take a disaster school and turn it around in just one year?" When I said it was our weight training program, they would ask me to come to their schools and show them how to do it. That was how our BFS clinics began, and those schools that I worked with also saw dramatic turnarounds in their programs.

In between my football jobs in Washington and Idaho, I was hired as the strength coach at Brigham Young University. At BYU I did a movie called *Bigger Faster Stronger*. The movie was a hit, and the secret was out nationwide. Football coaches nationwide began doing the BFS program, but even so, it seemed to be a slow process. In addition, coaches from other sports just could not get it.

In December of 1981, I was hired by the Utah Jazz to be their strength coach. At that time I was the only strength coach in the National Basketball Association (NBA). BFS was with the Utah Jazz for 16 years.

Professional baseball did not start hiring strength coaches until the 1990s. Even today, if you took all the high school athletes in the United States, male and female, you would still find that fewer than half possess the key to becoming bigger, faster, and stronger. It's simple—if you want to make success happen and unlock your full potential as an athlete, you must use the key.

Today, about 95 percent of college strength coaches use the methods I learned from George in one form or another. The remaining 5 percent focus on a different approach, with injury prevention as the primary goal instead of winning and performance. The BFS program will certainly help prevent injuries by preparing the body to withstand the stresses involved in sport training and competition, but BFS goals go far beyond that. We constantly measure performance. How fast can you run? How high and far can you jump? How much can you lift? How much can you improve in those areas? Personal records are meticulously kept in order to verify that improvement. That is what drives throwers and most other athletes. We need concrete proof that we are getting better every day. As for injuries, we have countless testimonials from schools that show dramatic decreases in injuries both in the weight room and on the playing field from implementing the BFS program.

STEFAN FERNHOLM: THE SOVIET CONNECTION

The third major contributor to the BFS program was Stefan Fernholm, a discus thrower from Sweden who came to BYU to compete at the college level. He broke the National Collegiate Athletic Association (NCAA) record and was a past Olympian. Stefan became a part of BFS in the mid-1980s. We owe him a great deal for bridging the gap between the United States and the former Soviet Union. Stefan was knowledgeable about the Soviet training methods. The Soviets took their training seriously, spending hundreds of millions of dollars developing their system. Their coaches, for example, could get a doctorate in discus, sprinting, or weightlifting at the University of Moscow. In the early 1970s they were discreetly building on their methods and elevating them to new levels.

Stefan took full advantage of this knowledge. I have never seen an athlete like him. Those of you who were able to see Stefan know I'm not blowing smoke. Stefan weighed 273 pounds (124 kilograms) at a little over 6 feet, 1 inch (185 centimeters) in height. He could run a legitimate 4.3-second 40-yard (37-meter) dash, vertical jump 40 inches

(102 centimeters) from a stand, and power clean 476 pounds (216 kilograms) from the floor. Stefan was flawless in everything he did. This is what he brought to the BFS table: Perfect technique! All our clinicians, including me, became better coaches and much greater technicians because of Stefan. Perfection became our focus. By all means, know all the secrets, but you had better execute every facet perfectly to put it all together. Stefan demonstrated this perfect technique in many of our videos. Unfortunately, Stefan died in Sweden several years ago, but his legacy lives on in BFS.

BFS TODAY

The next step was putting all these unique elements into a unified program for coaches and their athletes. It was not an easy task, considering that some sports such as track are individual sports, and throwers, for example, traditionally could train only themselves and maybe one or two others at the same time. The Soviet coaches I had observed would get nervous if they had to coach more than three athletes at a time. My own challenge for BFS was to figure out a way to implement the basic elements of advanced training used by athletes such as Stefan and put them into a package that could be used by multiple teams at the same time.

This book will guide you step by step on how to implement the BFS program, whether you are a coach training a team or an individual athlete training by yourself. The first three parts of the book focus on the workout program: the total program, strength exercises, and speed, agility, and flexibility. It's best to read these chapters in the order presented, acquiring a solid grasp of the BFS training principles before focusing on the performance of the strength and conditioning chapters. The final chapter is written primarily for coaches and school administrators, but it contains information that would be valuable for athletes to understand.

Now, with solid research, 30 years of practical knowledge, and tens of thousands of athletes using the program, we think we've got it right. The BFS program is the perfect program for any high school athlete, male or female, and it's ideal for coaches who deal with large numbers of athletes. The program also has shown remarkable success at the college level. Why not join the BFS team and make memories you'll be proud to share?

PART I

The Total Program

CHAPTER 1

Unified Approach to Training

One of the unique aspects of the Bigger Faster Stronger (BFS) program, and the one that can turn struggling athletic programs into winning programs, is unification. Unification is the concept that all high school athletes, and most college athletes for that matter, should adhere to the same basic training philosophy. This means that all athletes, from football players to basketball players to swimmers, should perform the same core weight training exercises, the same speed and agility exercises, and the same flexibility and plyometric exercises.

At BFS, we believe that all high school and most college athletes should be unified. Such organization reduces teaching time, prevents many administrative hassles and personality conflicts, and improves athletic performance. In today's world of budget cuts and reduced staffs, having all athletes use the same workout program year-round reduces the amount of time needed for teaching new exercises and training programs. The days of 40-hour work weeks for coaches may be over. To avoid staff burnout and handle frequent shuffling of teachers and coaches among schools, administrators need to focus on programs that are simple and versatile.

One of the worst problems for the multisport athlete is having each coach prescribe a different strength and conditioning program. We've visited many high schools where the football coach did an intense program primarily with free weights and the girls basketball coach did little strength training with free weights, using primarily machines. The girls' coach would say, "My girls are intimidated by free weights," and would therefore limit their strength training to inferior exercises. The baseball coach would tell players, "Weights will make you muscle bound," and would have them do no strength training whatsoever.

A high school may have as many as seven separate strength training programs! The same goes for each area of training: warm-up, speed, endurance, agility, plyometrics, and flexibility. Ignoring some of the preceding areas in a conditioning program is even a coaching philosophy for some. For example, the baseball coach who does not make strength training an integral part of the in-season program and who never works with the athletes on running faster sends a negative message to the players.

Territorial struggles among coaches unnecessarily test the loyalty of the athlete. The result is that coaches often force athletes to participate in only one sport, which adversely affects the quality of the school's athletic program. The unnecessary tension among coaching staffs is often the rule rather than the exception for high schools and small colleges.

When coaches adopt the BFS system, all athletes perform the same basic program throughout the entire school year and during the summer. Confusion disappears, coaches enjoy a spirit of teamwork with their colleagues, and athletes more easily achieve their goals. That's why it's no surprise to us when an athletic program does an immediate turnaround after we've set up a unified program at a BFS clinic.

In the BFS system, all athletes perform the same basic program throughout the entire year.

ELEMENTARY AND HIGH SCHOOL PROGRAMS

At BFS clinics we go beyond simply teaching reps, sets, and exercises. Our clinicians teach coaches and administrators how to unify their athletic program so that it encompasses all sports for both male and female athletes, grades 7 through 12. And to keep the terminology simple, we give the school the option of referring to it as the BFS total program or naming it after their school mascot. Let's say the team mascot is a tiger. Everyone does the Tiger stretching program. The Tigers would also have unified speed, warm-up, endurance, agility, plyometric, and weight training programs. It's that simple—and it works!

With unification, a two- or three-sport Tiger athlete would move smoothly from sport season to sport season without interruption. Let's take the example of a football player who is also on the basketball team. After the football season, this athlete would not have to wait four to six weeks to get started on a basketball-specific strength training program. He would just stay on the Tigers' in-season program. Athletes don't have a Tiger basketball in-season program; they just have the Tiger in-season program. This approach makes the coaches' job easier because they don't have to waste time teaching new lifting exercises. Also, the same warm-up (for example, the BFS dot drill) and flexibility exercises naturally continue. It's what the Tigers do!

Middle school athletes would follow the same guidelines. After they learn proper technique, seventh graders can do the same workouts that high school athletes do. Because competition at the high school level continues to reach higher standards, athletes must get into the weight room as soon as possible so that they don't fall behind. Just think of the advantages when those young kids who are maturing and developing with the Tiger total program get to high school!

Bob Giesey has been a coach and athletic director at American Heritage Academy in Carrollton, Texas. Since 1985 he has started his athletes on the BFS program as early as third grade (a group he calls the *ankle biters*). He came up with several benefits of getting elementary school athletes involved in BFS:

Develops competitive spirit through physical drills

Provides excellent physical conditioning

Develops a working attitude

Teaches discipline that will have a positive effect on daily living and academics

Builds teamwork

Develops personality

Increases confidence

Creates a sense of belonging to a group

Improves communication, which in turn improves trust

Teaches responsibility, which in turn improves caring for others and equipment

Allows athletes to see how hard others are working to reach objectives

Teaches respect

Develops enthusiasm individually and as a group

Teaches athletes to dream to achieve

Teaches the value of commitment

Helps athletes be organized (dress, equipment, and so on)

Develops good decision-making skills

Teaches promptness

Promotes participation in middle school and high school sport

Permits an easy transition from grade school to middle school to high school

COLLEGE PROGRAMS

Many Division I schools have outstanding sport-conditioning programs, and in every issue of our magazine, *Bigger Faster Stronger,* we profile the best college programs. But it would be presumptuous to suggest that the BFS program is better than the program at Oklahoma or Miami or any other Division I school. I will say, however, that most Division II, Division III, National Association of Intercollegiate Athletics (NAIA), and junior college programs would be successful with the total BFS program simply because it more fully addresses those particular situations and athletes. The BFS program is also easy for coaches to implement, which is especially important for small colleges that do not have full-time strength coaches to develop specific programs for each sport.

What if Division I athletes miss workouts? They might lose a scholarship. What about high school athletes? The BFS program is designed to create massive voluntary participation with daily increases of self-confidence; the athletes want to train hard and not miss workouts. The BFS system also flows easily from one sport to the next and unifies all sports into an easily managed total strength and conditioning program.

One example of the effectiveness of unification is the program that Roger VanDeZande ran at Southern Oregon University (SOU). VanDeZande, who was also the defensive coordinator for football, was responsible for supervising the conditioning programs of more than 250 athletes in numerous sports. VanDeZande used the BFS program at the high school level and knew that he would be working with a large number of athletes when he went to SOU. He saw no reason to change his coaching philosophy. "When I look at many of the teams we've hammered despite their superior talent and facilities, it's obvious that if they were doing what they should be doing they would beat us," says VanDeZande.

UNIFICATION MANAGEMENT

Although more than a million athletes have used the BFS program, less than 2 percent of all high schools in America have adopted a true unified program. This means that more than 17,000 high schools do not implement their strength and conditioning programs correctly. Unification offers many advantages over other programs, and it's why coaches from all sports enthusiastically accept our presentations at BFS clinics.

Although equipment considerations are discussed later in this book, we strongly recommend using two products to build a quality, unified program that will help all athletes in all sports. First is a lightweight Olympic barbell that weighs 15 pounds (7 kilograms), along with 5- and 10-pound (2- and 5-kilogram) Olympic-size training plates. Teaching Olympic lifting exercises is much easier with this equipment, because the barbell with weights can weigh as little as 25 pounds (11 kilograms). Athletes can concentrate on technique because they won't worry about the weight or be forced to bend too low with smaller plates.

Next is detailed record keeping in the form of personal logbooks or a computer spreadsheet program. Keeping records helps athletes set daily goals, and they receive positive reinforcement when they see their long-term progress in print.

Logbooks work well in any situation. For larger programs, a quality software program is a good way to keep track of hundreds of athletes. John Hoch is the head football coach at Lancaster High School in Lancaster, Wisconsin. After the Lancaster football team compiled a 41–1 record in three years, Coach Hoch's story appeared in *BFS* magazine. In that interview, he praised our computer system, Beat the Computer. "Beat the Computer has made my job unbelievably easier," said Hoch. "You can print out the program by specific sports, which is really great because more and more of our kids are getting involved with weights."

Coach Hoch also found that our computer program helped motivate his athletes to train harder: "Our kids are always pushing themselves on their final sets, but the Beat the Computer program pushed them on their first and second sets—or if it's a long program, on the first through the fourth sets. This made the final set really a challenge. It really made a difference in getting our athletes strong."

The BFS program combines the best of strength and conditioning from all over the world. The system recognizes the great differences among elite, pro, and college athletes compared with those at the high school level. The BFS program is perfect for large numbers of athletes, block schedules, middle schools, in-season and off-season transitions, and multisport athletes, and it creates great self-confidence and massive voluntary participation.

Unification: It just makes sense!

Logansport High School

Logansport High School earned the 2006 BFS High School of the Year award for all the Logansport athletic teams.

"United we stand, divided we fall" is an expression that dates back to as early as Aesop's fables from sixth century BC. Its emotional appeal has been used in countless speeches to inspire people to work as a team to achieve common goals. "United we stand, divided we fall" is an appropriate motto for what has taken place in the athletic programs at Logansport High School in Logansport, Indiana. And it's their mission to inspire all their athletes to succeed that earned Logansport the title of 2006 BFS High School of the Year.

One of the most dramatic examples of the weight training payoff is football. Logansport has been using the BFS program for the past four years and turned around a 1-9 team to subsequent records of 5-6, 11-3 and 10-1. But the Logansport Berries' athletic turnaround extends beyond football.

The boys basketball team rose from cellar dwellers to conference contenders, and the wrestling program recently won its first sectional title since 2000. The gymnastics girls have been ranked in the top 10 for the past two years, with several achieving the highest individual scores in the state. All the cheerleaders can tumble, and many of them compete in other sports. "Overall, the BFS system has been an integral part of the success of our high school," says Coach Kramer.

Just how unified is the Berries' success? Here is a breakdown of the school's teams that finished with winning records:

Basketball, boys (16–7)	*Baseball* (15–12)
Baseball (15–12)	*Soccer,* boys (12–7–1)
Cross country, boys (5–4)	*Swimming,* girls (13–1)
Cross country, girls (6–3)	*Tennis,* girls (16–5)
Golf, girls (9–4)	*Track,* girls (8–1)
Gymnastics (13–0)	*Wrestling* (17–7)

When asked what he liked about the workout, Kramer replied, "The BFS program involves a unified program for high school athletes. With BFS you're lifting in-season, continually seeing improvement—you never plateau." And at Logansport, Kramer says that girls are treated as equals in regards to lifting.

Kramer says that at first there were concerns among the athletes and parents about having girls lift weights the same as the guys, but "when they were given the physiological proof that a girl cannot get as big as a guy, they understood." It also helped them to see many female athletes lifting heavy without bulking up. Now, not only are the girls OK with lifting, but many have embraced it, notes Kramer, adding that recently a cheerleader deadlifted 350 pounds (159 kilograms)!

Logansport has developed a support system in which athletes are encouraged to participate in multiple sports. He also says that the regular physical education classes use aspects of the BFS program so that students who decide to try out for a sport the following year won't be far behind in their conditioning. "We've been able to pull many kids from those nonathletic weight training classes into our athletic program," says Kramer.

A final ingredient in the Logansport athletic program is a focus on character education, which Kramer says incorporates many aspects of the Be an Eleven program (covered in chapter 18). "We stay positive with our kids. Some of our athletic programs may struggle at times, but everyone here is striving for the same thing—to excel at whatever we do!"

CHAPTER 2

BFS Rotational Set–Rep System

"The best workout program is the one you are not using," is a popular expression in the field of strength and conditioning. In a sense this is true. Many workout programs fail because their exercise prescriptions are so monotonous that the body adapts to them and is therefore no longer stimulated to make progress. However, this is not the case with the Bigger Faster Stronger (BFS) rotational set–rep system, a proven training program that rotates the weekly set–rep prescriptions so that athletes can set records on a daily basis.

Athletes will always be in a position to make continual progress and break personal records every workout with the BFS program. No other program can do this. When athletes do three sets of 10 reps, one set of 15, or five sets of 5, they reach plateaus quickly. To break personal records every workout, you must continually alternate all the major training variables, including exercises, reps, and sets.

The BFS system allows you to alternate exercises, sets, and reps in such a way that you repeat a specific workout only every fifth week. This system has two simple rules: First, establish your records, and second, break those records. If you follow this system exactly, you will never reach a plateau.

Being able to break records frequently is extremely motivating, especially for young athletes. Although older athletes may be satisfied with breaking a personal record for a lift once a month, younger athletes are often impatient and quickly lose interest in such a program. The

BFS program is set up so that there are several opportunities to break personal records, including the amount of weight lifted, the number of reps performed in an exercise, and the total number of reps performed in a workout. It's possible that athletes could break a dozen records in a single workout, but even if they are having an off day it is still possible to break at least one record.

Two more important advantages of the BFS rotational set–rep system are that it is simple to use and can be implemented easily with a large number of athletes. Such versatility makes the BFS program perfect for high schools and small colleges, most of which do not have the financial and personnel resources of Division I college programs.

Countless athletes at thousands of high schools have used the BFS rotational set–rep system over the past 32 years. Andy Griffin, a highly successful Texas high school football coach, gave us a typical response after implementing the program: "When is this going to stop? I mean, can they keep breaking records like this? My athletes have broken so many records these past months, I can't believe it. Thanks!" Yes, they will keep breaking records. We guarantee eight new personal records per week for as long as the athletes are in high school.

OVERCOMING PLATEAUS

With any form of strength and conditioning, athletes experience plateaus, or a leveling off or even a dropping off in performance. Athletes can become frustrated, depressed, and ready to quit because of this phenomenon. Leveling off happens to everyone, but there are ways to prolong upward movement and overcome plateaus.

In 1946, endocrinologist Hans Selye introduced a theory of how the body responds to stress. He explained this theory in a model he called the *general adaptation syndrome* (GAS). Selye found that when people are subjected to any kind of stress, they go through all or part of the phases outlined in the model. The phases are commonly referred to as shock, countershock, stage of resistance, and stage of exhaustion. The BFS rotational set–rep system is based on Selye's model (figure 2.1).

Using the stages described in the GAS, a young woman goes outside and is ready to jump into an unheated pool. Her friends say, "Come on in. The water's fine once you get used to it." So she jumps in. First she's in shock, but then she starts to get used to it. That's countershock. Soon she is jumping in and out and having a great time. This is the stage of resistance. Eventually, depending on the temperature of the water, she will start to freeze and will even die if she stays in. This final stage, exhaustion, usually happens quickly. In two-a-day practices, for example, most athletes reach the stage of resistance by the fifth or sixth

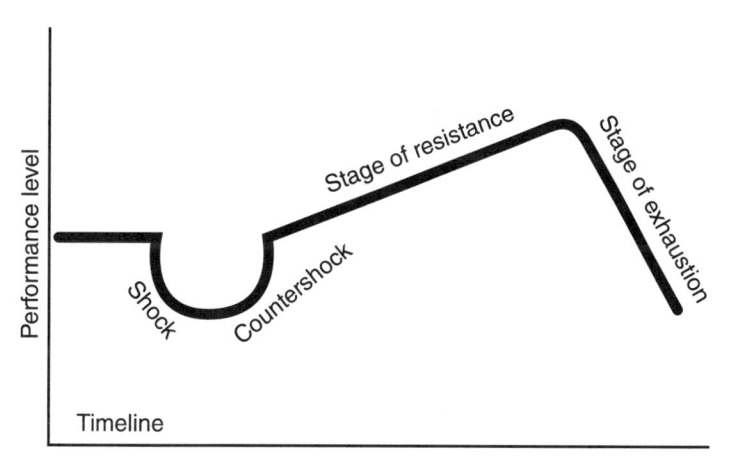

FIGURE 2.1 Hans Selye's stress theory.

day. The problem is how to prolong the stage of resistance throughout the entire season and not enter the stage of exhaustion.

Selye's GAS model can easily be applied to sets and reps in weight training. If an athlete performs three sets of 10 reps every day with the same exercises, the stage of exhaustion will occur in about four weeks. The same would be true of one set of 8 to 12 reps or five sets of 5 reps.

To avoid going into the exhaustion stage, athletes must vary the sets, reps, and exercises on a weekly basis. Every time a variation is inserted into the program, the stage of resistance is prolonged. The BFS rotational set–rep system offers a great deal of variation. Every day is different; a given workout occurs only every fifth week. The system of breaking records is highly motivational, and the weekly variety in sets and reps helps prolong the resistance stage. Here are some other ways to keep athletes disciplined and working hard:

- Use charts for motivation and design them so that everyone feels successful.
- Regularly set dates for competitions against other athletes or schools or for new maximums.
- Use motivational films and stories.
- Use awards such as T-shirts and certificates.
- Vary time, place, days, partners, sequence, intensity, or diet.
- Increase diet, sleep, or rest.
- When athletes return after a layoff, have them forget all past achievements and start an all-new set of records.

The challenge for coaches is to find the optimal balance between regularity of routine and appropriate variations that will enable athletes to make continual progress and avoid plateaus. By using programs such as the BFS rotational set–rep system that prolong the stage of resistance, coaches will undoubtedly prolong their coaching tenure.

PERIODIZATION OR BFS?

For high school athletes, especially those who play more than one sport, the BFS rotational set–rep system is superior to the most sophisticated periodization systems used by many European countries. This is because the BFS system flows perfectly from one sport season to the next and is ideal for a team approach. But the BFS system can also work well for single-sport athletes because the Tuesday–Thursday program develops speed, agility, and overall athleticism. These are bold statements, so let's analyze why they are true.

Periodization is dividing an annual plan of training into phases to attain peaks during the most important competitions. Some people categorize these phases as preparation, competition, and transition. These phases are normally broken down into subphases called *macrocycles* or *microcycles*. Each cycle varies the sets, reps, exercises, and training intensity (i.e., the amount of weight lifted).

On the surface, the periodization cycles used by elite athletes in the former Eastern Bloc countries seem to have great merit. Many top universities espouse periodization. So why shouldn't high schools do the same? Here are five reasons:

1. Training teams. Periodization was originally intended for individuals. Many universities train their athletes in small groups, whereas high school athletes usually train as a team so that coaches can organize the workout as they would a practice. With the BFS system, the intensity levels of teams and individuals can reach incredible heights because it's possible for all athletes to see progress on a daily basis, and their enthusiasm for their success becomes contagious.

2. Peaking for competitions. When do you peak in a periodization program? Do you choose to peak for homecoming, the conference championship, or the playoffs? In many periodization programs, you would peak for one major contest each year. In American football, you had better have some sort of peak every week, or you won't have to worry about peaking for the play-offs.

3. Training the multisport athlete. Universities and Eastern European national programs normally deal only with one-sport athletes. Administering a periodization program for a large group of high school athletes would be a nightmare. For example, after the football season, let's say 15 of the 65 players go into basketball, 20 go out for wrestling, and the remaining 30 are in an off-season program. Then in March, 12 of the football players who play basketball go out for a spring sport; 7 go out for baseball and 5 go out for track. The other 3 basketball–football players join the off-season program. The 30 kids who were in the off-season program now split into groups. Twenty have decided to enter a spring sport. In the summer, 17 football players also play baseball, while others attend basketball, wrestling, and football camps. Got all that? Athletes would be running in and out of phases and cycles all year long, requiring many schedules and programs.

4. **Obtaining accurate maxes.** An athlete has a 175-pound (79-kilogram) clean, and he's supposed to train with 60 percent at 105 pounds (48 kilograms), 70 percent at 122.5 pounds (56 kilograms), 80 percent at 140 pounds (64 kilograms), and so on. Yet after the athlete goes to a BFS clinic and learns about intensity and technique, he will typically clean 225 pounds (102 kilograms). So now what? In all probability, much of his training with 110 and 130 pounds (50 and 59 kilograms) during an eight-week periodization cycle was unproductive because the weights were too light. The percentage system used in most periodization programs doesn't account for the variety in the athlete's training state. Some days the athlete may be a bit down in strength, and as a result the weights prescribed would be too heavy and technique could be compromised as the athlete attempts to lift weights he is not ready for, especially in the power clean and other quick lifts. Some days the athlete may be capable of lifting much heavier weights, so the weights prescribed would be too light and as a result the athlete would not get the optimal training stimulus to become stronger.

5. **Making rapid progress.** The BFS rotational set–rep system provides intense, challenging, and motivating training sessions. Periodization programs don't allow for daily variance in strength. The BFS system corrects itself on a set basis during the workout. Athletes don't have to wait for a long time to break a record. On the BFS system they break records every workout. Periodization can hold high school teams back because the weights prescribed are often too light or too heavy, whereas the BFS system propels teams forward week after week at breakneck speed.

It's true that we've borrowed selectively from periodization and Eastern European systems. We've packaged the most appropriate training practices into a system that works amazingly well for high school athletes involved in team sports while taking into consideration their time and logistics constraints. Let your competition try to sort out all the research and come up with a periodization program. Let your competition copy the system of a Russian weightlifter. Let your competition use a university program and scramble to adapt it to the high school situation.

Meanwhile, with the progressive and reliable BFS system, you'll be getting all the results you've been looking for.

THE WORKOUT

The BFS system for off-season training is set up on four-week cycles, with each week consisting of the following core lifts performed on specific days. Although the order of the lifts remains the same, each week you will use a different set–rep prescription for the core lifts. Table 2.1 outlines what training components are emphasized each workout day and table 2.2 illustrates the four-week cycle.

Record keeping is especially important with the BFS rotational set–rep system because you often break records every training day, making it easy to lose track of your progress without some type of logbook. How do you know if you are improving if you don't write down what you've done in the past? Many coaches use teachers' aides to assist the athletes.

Now let's go through the core lifts and set–rep schemes for an entire training cycle, starting with week 1, Monday.

Monday, Week 1 (3 × 3)

This first workout may seem too easy, but keep in mind that the main concern here is making sure that you follow the proper spotting and lifting techniques.

- **Box squat.** On the first set, select between 45 and 145 pounds (20 and 66 kilograms) for three reps. For the second set, you may either go up in poundage, stay the same, or go down. For example, if you feel good about 145 pounds (66 kilograms), you can go up to 175 pounds (79 kilograms) on your second set and then 205 pounds (93 kilograms) for the third set. On the final set, you should do 3 or more reps, up to 10 reps if you can.

Table 2.1 BFS Total Program

Monday	Tuesday	Wednesday	Thursday	Friday
Squat variation	Sprint work	Power clean	Sprint work	Parallel squat
Bench variation	Plyometrics	Hex bar	Plyometrics	Bench press
Auxiliary lifts	Flexibility	Auxiliary lifts	Flexibility	Auxiliary lifts
Flexibility	Agility	Flexibility	Agility	Flexibility
Agility	Technique	Agility	Technique	Agility

Table 2.2	Four-Week Training Cycle
Week 1	The first week is easy. After warm-ups, do 3 × 3. On the last set, do 3 more. Give an all-out effort!
Week 2	Do 5 × 5 or, if you have only 45 minutes of class time, cut it down to 3 × 5. Doing 5 × 5 is difficult, even brutal. On the last set, do 5 more. Again, give your all.
Week 3	Do 5-4-3-2-1 or, if time is a problem, do 5-3-1. This is moderately difficult. On the last set, do 1 or more.
Week 4	Establish another set record and records for more reps. Do 10-8-6 on the bench, towel bench, squat, and box squat, and do 4-4-2 on the clean and deadlift or hex-bar lift. *Important concept:* Do 6 or more reps on the last set, depending on the core lift.
Week 5	Start the rotation over with the workout for week 1. Do more weight than in week 1 and break more set and rep records.

The reps and sets outlined above *do not* include warm-up sets and are not necessarily relevant to all core lifts or auxiliary exercises. For example, a set-rep scheme of 4-4-2 (4 reps, 4 reps, 2 reps) is prescribed on week 4 for the power clean and the hex-bar deadlift because it's difficult to maintain perfect form on those exercises with higher reps.

- **Towel bench.** If you know your max on the bench, take 70 percent of your max for your first set (or two-thirds of your max). For example, if your max is 200 pounds (91 kilograms), begin with 140 pounds (64 kilograms) for three reps on your first set. If you've never done benches before, use 70 percent of your body weight or 105 pounds (48 kilograms), whichever is less. If this is too much weight for three reps, use 60 percent or even 50 percent of your body weight. The more experience an athlete has with the BFS program, the easier it will become to determine the appropriate warm-up weights—and most athletes will know after their first warm-up set if they are capable to establishing a personal record that day. For your second set, you may go up, stay the same, or go down. Do three or more reps on the final set, but on this first workout select a weight that you can do 10 times. If possible, you want to establish your rep records for all lifts you will record.

Now it's time to record your results. Say your results were as follows:

Box squat: 145 + 175 + 205 = 525 pounds
(66 + 79 + 93 = 238 kilograms)

Towel bench: 140 + 150 + 150 = 440 pounds
(64 + 68 + 68 = 200 kilograms)

- **Establish set and rep records.** The total amount of weight lifted is your set record. In the example, the box squat set record is 525 pounds (238 kilograms) and the towel bench set record is 440 pounds (200 kilograms). In the sample training log in figure 2.4, notice the box labeled *actual reps.* This is where you will record the reps you made on your last set.

For your rep record, follow this example. Let's say you did 10 reps at 205 pounds (93 kilograms) on the box squat and 10 reps at 150 pounds (68 kilograms) on the towel bench on the final set. Record your box squat and towel bench rep records. Simply write in the weight lifted for the correct number of reps and write the date in the box at the upper right (figures 2.2 and 2.3). Figure 2.4 is an example of how to record your success for the towel bench.

FIGURE 2.2 This is an example of establishing rep records.

FIGURE 2.3 This is an example of establishing rep records.

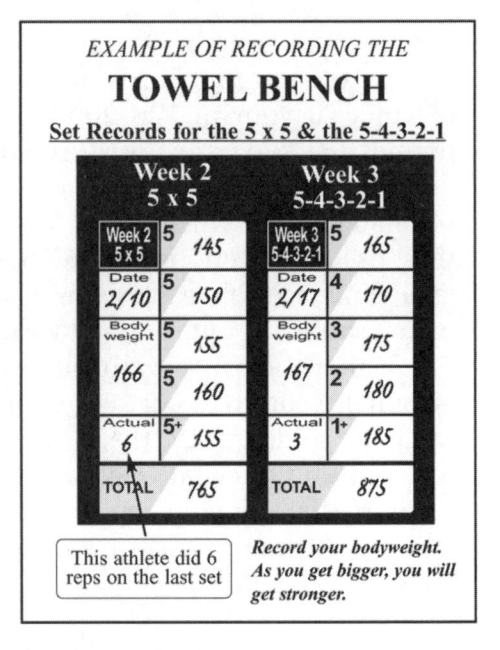

FIGURE 2.4 This is an example of recording the towel bench.

Wednesday, Week 1 (3 × 3)

- **Power clean.** Do the 3 × 3 workout. Use 70 percent of your maximum, or about two-thirds of your best. If you've never cleaned before, use 70 percent of your body weight or 105 pounds (48 kilograms), whichever is less. Use the same procedure for the second and third sets (as in Monday's workout) and record your efforts. On the final set, you should do three or more reps, up to five reps. Try to do five reps.
- **Hex-bar deadlift.** Do the 3 × 3 workout. Start with 145 pounds (66 kilograms) or your body weight, whichever is less. Follow the same procedure and record your efforts. Again, on the final set, you should do three or more reps, up to five reps.

Friday, Week 1 (3 × 3)

- **Bench press and squat.** Do the 3 × 3 workout. Use the poundage and procedures that you used in Monday's towel bench and box squat workouts.

Week 2 (5 × 5)

Do five sets of five reps (5 × 5). This is a long, brutal workout. You may wish to cut it down to three sets of five because of time or your energy level, especially on the hex-bar and clean day. Select your poundage as you did in the first week. Record your efforts. You should do five or more reps on the last set except when doing the clean or hex bar.

Week 3 (5-4-3-2-1)

Do 5-4-3-2-1. This workout is not quite as hard as 5 × 5, but you may want to cut it down to 5-3-1 because of time constraints or your energy level. In figure 2.5, 165 pounds (75 kilograms) were lifted for five reps, 170 pounds (77 kilograms) for four reps, 185 pounds (84 kilograms) for three reps, and so on. Record your efforts. You will establish your 5-4-3-2-1 set records, and you should be breaking some rep records as illustrated. Do one or more reps on the last set.

EXAMPLE OF RECORDING THE

REP RECORDS

A Established Records in 1st 3 x 3 Week
B Broken Records in 5 x 5 Week
C Broken Records in 5-4-3-2-1 Week
D Broken Records in 4th Week
E Broken Records in Week 5

REP RECORDS

REP	Establish Records	1st Break	2nd Break	3rd Break
1	A 2/3 150	B 2/10 160	C 2/17 185	E 3/3 190
2	A 2/3 150	B 2/10 160	C 2/17 185	E 3/3 190
3	A 2/3 150	B 2/10 160	C 2/17 185	E 3/3 190
4	A 2/3 150	B 2/10 160	C 2/17 170	E 3/3 190
5	A 2/3 150	B 2/10 160	C 2/17 165	Date Weight
6	A 2/3 150	B 2/10 155	D 2/24 160	Date Weight
8	A 2/3 150	D 2/24 160	Date Weight	Date Weight
10	A 2/3 150	D 2/24 160	Date Weight	Date Weight

FIGURE 2.5 This is an example of recording rep records.

The third week is a perfect time to max out on a one-rep max just by following the regular routine. Or, once every three months you could go 5-3-1 to prevent fatigue at the last set. Another option is to take 10 to 20 pounds (5-9 kilograms) off your 5-4-3-2 rep maxes and then do several singles on the way to a long one-rep max.

Week 4 (10-8-6 or 4-4-2)

Do 10-8-6. You will notice that the rep records go to only five reps on the clean and the hex bar or deadlift. Doing extra reps on those two lifts could cause an injury, especially to the lower back. As fatigue sets in, you increase the chances of incurring muscle spasms and failing to maintain correct lifting technique.

Week 5 (Starting Over, 3 × 3)

Now the fun of the BFS system really begins! From now on, every time you come into the weight room, you have a challenge and an objective. You should try to break as many set and rep records as possible. Begin week 5 by again doing the 3 × 3 workout. The objective is simply to do more!

Look what happened in the example of the fifth week (3 × 3) for the towel bench—five new records! The athlete smashed the set record (total) by 100 pounds (45 kilograms), going from 440 total pounds (200 kilograms) to 540 pounds (245 kilograms). In addition, four new rep records were attained (three standard reps plus one extra rep). Refer to the rep record chart example. Under the third break column, 190 pounds (86 kilograms) should be recorded along with the date for the 3 × 3. Many athletes like to try to break their 10-rep record after doing 3 × 3, because this is an easy week. We call this a *burnout set*.

Weeks 6, 7, and 8 (5 × 5, 5-4-3-2-1, Then 10-8-6 or 4-4-2)

Break as many rep records as you can! On week 6 break your 5 × 5 set record, on week 7 break your 5-4-3-2-1 set record, and on week 8 break your 10-8-6 set record. If you are trying for a new six-rep max on week 8 and still have power to spare when you get to the sixth rep, don't stop. Squeeze out as many reps as you can (up to 10). The same goes for the clean and hex bar with the 4-4-2. If you are going for a new two-rep max and still have power for more reps, do it! Be intense. Remember, each additional rep is a new record. Want to win? Break a record.

Now keep rotating your workouts in the four-week cycle. You can expect to break 8 or more records per week or 400 per year for as long as you want. Each of the six core lifts has four set records (3-3-5,-5 and 5-4-3-2-1), so that's 24 possible set records. The bench press, towel bench, squat, and box squat each have 8 rep records, and the hex bar

Helpful Hints

1. "Or more" means the number of reps up to 10 on the bench, towel bench, squat, and box squat and up to 5 reps on the clean and hex bar.
2. Call attention to athletes breaking records. Dothan High School in Alabama has a bell at each station. When an athlete is going for a record, the bell is rung. This practice really seems to increase the intensity.
3. Many coaches use teachers' aides to assist the athletes with record keeping.
4. Changing the sequence of the lifts can help overcome a plateau (for example, the athlete can do the bench first instead of the squat).

or deadlift and the clean each have 5 rep records, which makes 42 possible rep records, or a total of 66 possible records. When you count the auxiliary lifts and performance tests, you have even more records. That's why it is easy to break so many records.

Remember, we are not concerned with breaking only a one-rep max; we want to break all kinds of rep records. We know, for example, that if we break a three-rep record, the max will also go up soon.

FINER POINTS

- **Warm-ups.** Table 2.3 is your guideline to warm-ups. If you can lift over 200 pounds (91 kilograms) for any exercise, you need to do warm-up sets to prepare the muscles and nervous system for the heavy work to come—you just can't go into a gym and break a personal record without physical and psychological preparation. You usually perform

Table 2.3 Warm-Up Guidelines

Routine	Warm-up
>200 lb	0-1 set
200-295 lb	1-2 sets
300-395 lb	2-3 sets
400-495 lb	3-4 sets
500-595 lb	4-5 sets

these warm-up sets for five reps, and you don't record them in your set–rep logbook. For example:

> 3 × 3 with 275 pounds (125 kilograms); warm up with 195 and 235 pounds (88 and 107 kilograms)
>
> 5 × 5 with 330 pounds (150 kilograms); warm up with 235 and 295 pounds (107 and 134 kilograms)
>
> 5-4-3-2-1 with 450 pounds (204 kilograms); warm up with 235, 325, and 415 pounds (107, 147, and 188 kilograms)

Notice that all the rep records are the same at this time. Don't worry about that. The numbers will change rapidly as you break your rep records, which will normally happen every workout.

- **Missing a rep.** Sometimes you may miss a rep. For example, you're trying to do 3 × 3 with 275 pounds (125 kilograms) and on the last set you can only do two reps. You have two options: rest and try again with the same or a lighter weight or penalize yourself 5 pounds (2 kilograms) per 100 pounds (45 kilograms) on the bar. (This is not an exact science, but the important idea is to establish a consistent penalty system for missed attempts.)

For example, in the previous situation you're penalized 10 pounds (5 kilograms), so add 275 + 275 + 265 pounds (125 + 125 + 120 kilograms) for your total. If you're lifting in the 500-pound (227-kilogram) range, your penalty would be 25 pounds (11 kilograms) for missing one rep and 50 pounds (23 kilograms) for missing two reps. See table 2.4 for penalties.

- **Adjusting.** The BFS system gives you flexibility in adjusting poundage as you progress through your workout. For example, your 3 × 3 set record is 1,095 pounds (497 kilograms). So you do your first set with 370 pounds (168 kilograms), and it's easy. For your second set you select 390 pounds (177 kilograms), and it's super tough. Therefore, on your third set, you bring it back down to 370 pounds (168 kilograms). Your new set record total is 1,130 pounds (513 kilograms).

Table 2.4 Penalty Table

Range	Penalty	Range	Penalty
100-195 lb	5 lb	400-495 lb	20 lb
200-295 lb	10 lb	500-595 lb	25 lb
300-395 lb	15 lb	600-695 lb	30 lb

- **Starting over.** You should start your records over after a layoff of four or more weeks, a major sickness, or a big drop in weight because your strength levels will be down. Also, football players should start over after two-a-days because these practices often create a state of overtraining that weakens the athlete.
- **Achieving records.** The BFS program includes 75 total records. There are 60 records up for grabs each week, plus 15 more if you count auxiliary exercises and performance records—the dot drill, sit-and-reach, 40- and 20-yard (37- and 18-meter) sprints, vertical jump, and standing long jump.

Being able to vary your workouts, record your lifts, and plan how to break your records are advantages built into the BFS program. Breaking records at a phenomenal rate is what makes the BFS program unique. We guarantee that athletes individually will break at least eight new personal records per week for as long as they are in high school, and the same would be true for a less experienced college athlete. What would happen if you broke eight personal records per week for one year? The idea almost boggles the mind, doesn't it? The sky is the limit!

CHAPTER 3

BFS In-Season Training

You are beginning the sport season. What do you do with weight training? If your answer is, "Wait until the off-season," you will inevitably lose the edge your athletes developed in the off-season. You must find time to weight train.

Let's say you have a football player who bench-pressed 250 pounds (113 kilograms) right before putting the pads on in August. If he does no weight training in the next few months, he will be benching 220 pounds (100 kilograms) by November 1, just when he needs to be the strongest. In contrast, if he did the BFS in-season program, he could possibly be benching 280 pounds (127 kilograms). This is not just an opinion. In addition to feedback from coaches who can vouch for the effectiveness of in-season training, several peer-reviewed research studies back up our evidence.

A weight training study published in the prestigious *Medicine and Science in Sports and Exercise* reported that subjects could retain their strength levels for up to 15 weeks even if they reduced the volume of work (total work) by two-thirds. The catch was that the intensity (heaviest total weight) had to be relatively high to achieve those results. Studies on aerobic conditioning have found the same results—it is much easier to retain conditioning with short but hard workouts than it is to regain it after a prolonged training layoff. To avoid overtraining while still progressing in all areas of physical conditioning, the Bigger Faster Stronger (BFS) system reduces the amount of work performed in-season while maintaining a high level of intensity.

IN-SEASON PROGRAM

If a team is used to training in the off-season and doesn't train during the in-season, the players will be mentally down at play-off time because of a perceived weakness. Conversely, if a team trains during the in-season, it will be confident for the play-offs and will be physically stronger than many teams who were stronger at the start of the season. What's better: being stronger at the beginning of the season or during the play-offs? Athletes simply must take the time to weight train. Here are the components of a successful in-season program.

- **Train twice per week.** During the sport season, one training session a week is not enough volume to make progress, and three training sessions are too draining. With the carefully selected exercises in the BFS program, you can even work out the day before the game without adversely affecting performance.
- **Train in the morning.** If possible, train before school or during a weight training class before lunch. There are many disadvantages to weight training just before or after practice. You'll get better results by getting up a half hour earlier to lift (a workout many coaches like to call *brawn at dawn*) than by trying to lift before or after practice.
- **Keep it to 30 minutes.** Keep in-season weight training workouts to 30 minutes or less. Remember, the objective of training is to win in your sport. You must focus a lot of time and energy on your sport during the season, and you simply cannot afford to spend many hours in the weight room. Two 30-minute sessions for a total of 1 hour during the week is sufficient, and it's amazing how much progress you can make in that time.
- **Emphasize the basic BFS core lifts.** You want to progress in the parallel squat, bench press, and clean throughout the season—you just can't let those go. However, you can skip many auxiliary exercises.

The beauty of performing the box squat during the in-season is that recovery occurs almost immediately. Research has shown that the lowering (i.e., eccentric) part of an exercise produces the most muscle damage, and the greater the range of motion, the more muscle mass is involved in the lift. The box squat focuses on the lifting (i.e., concentric) part of the exercise through a shorter range of motion so that athletes retain their strength without overtaxing their ability to recover. You can box squat heavy on Thursday and still play hard on Friday. To avoid overtraining, male athletes should generally keep the weight on the box squat within about 100 pounds (45 kilograms) of the parallel squat. Female athletes should stay within about 75 pounds (34 kilograms). Using heavier weights puts excessive compressive forces on the spine, making it difficult to perform the lift safely.

Likewise, the towel bench press is an effective in-season exercise because it keeps the stress level down while allowing some progress on the bench. The towel bench press puts much less stress on the shoulder joint than the regular bench press does, an important consideration in contact sports that punish the shoulders. You would do this lift on Wednesday or Thursday before the game.

You should perform the straight-leg deadlift with light weights during the season, no more than 30 percent of the parallel squat max. The straight-leg deadlift is primarily a stretching exercise to increase range of motion, so heavy weights are never used. Most high school athletes will therefore lift between 55 and 135 pounds (25 and 61 kilograms) for two sets of 10 reps. The primary objective of the straight-leg deadlift is to get a good hamstring and glute stretch while building strength in that area. Remember, this exercise is crucial to improving speed. You would not plug this exercise into the normal BFS set–rep routine because it is not considered a strength training exercise and thus it follows a different set–rep protocol.

Former Green Bay Packers football legend Reggie White performed box squats in-season to help him stay strong for every game.

- **Do only three big sets.** Just follow the BFS set–rep system during the season, as follows:
    - Week 1: 3 × 3
    - Week 2: 3 × 5
    - Week 3: 5-3-1 (a set of 5 reps, a set of 3 reps, and a set of 1 rep)
    - Week 4: 10-8-6 (and 4-2-2 for the clean and the hex-bar deadlift)

On week 5, repeat the week 1 workout, but challenge yourself to do more. Next, repeat the week 2 workout the same way, and so on. You will likely be able to get in three full cycles during a season.

ACHIEVING PROGRESS

Most college strength training programs try only to maintain strength levels during the season. At the high school level, you hope that your competition will adopt that practice. The philosophy of maintaining in college is acceptable because collegiate athletes often have a good base of strength and therefore will not lose much during the season. For example, a college football player benching 400 pounds (181 kilograms) will be happy with maintaining that level during the season. But the 16-year-old high school junior who is benching 200 pounds (91 kilograms) is still maturing and can easily gain strength during the season.

Another factor to consider is that a college athlete normally plays only one sport and has a long off-season. But what about that 16-year-old? What if he plays several sports? What's he going to do—just maintain all year? Let the competition stagnate. High school athletes should go for progress during the season and shouldn't be satisfied with simply maintaining.

One exception to in-season lifting concerns athletes who are in high-stress preseason training, such as football two-a-day practices. The kids are mentally and physically exhausted, and adding a lifting program in this situation creates too much stress.

Finally, consider that not all athletes have to be at peak conditioning during the in-season. Some athletes are red-shirted, and many freshmen will have little opportunity to play. Why not work those athletes harder in the weight room to give them a head start for the next year?

Mark Eaton, a former center for the Utah Jazz, broke 275 personal records during his rookie year using the BFS program. Mark later became an NBA all-star and two-time defensive player of the year. So get going! It's fun to get stronger. With BFS, athletes play better, feel better, and are more confident.

Strength Training Regimens: Joe, Deron, and Mike

Joe's football coach said, "We've got to practice, have meetings, and watch game films. We just don't have time to get in a strength workout." As a result, Joe lost most of the strength that he had built up over summer. When it came to basketball, Joe's coach said, "We have two games per week plus practices. If football can't lift in-season, we certainly can't." Joe's track coach said, "Weights will screw you up, so we ain't doin' nothin'."

Result? At the end of his freshman year, Joe was at about the same level of strength as he was in the eighth grade (figure 3.1). This same scenario occurred all four years. At graduation ceremonies, the coaches looked at Joe and said, "He was a good athlete. It's too bad he wasn't bigger, faster, and stronger. Why don't we ever get some mature-looking athletes?" The answer: lack of in-season weight training!

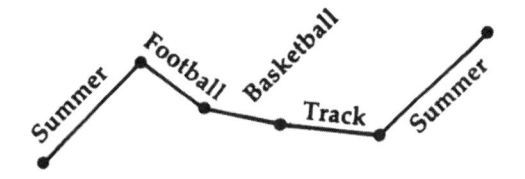

FIGURE 3.1 Joe's strength level.

Deron's football coach went to hear a strength coach from a major college talk about in-season training. "What we want to do is maintain!" said the expert. So that's what the high school coaches did during Deron's football, basketball, and track seasons throughout his high school career (figure 3.2). Deron spent all his life maintaining. The high school coaches didn't stop to think that the college situation was different. At that level, athletes play only one sport. Mature college athletes are satisfied with maintaining a 500-pound (227-kilogram) squat, 400-pound (181-kilogram) bench press, and 300-pound (136-kilogram) clean over one sport season. But at the high school level, most athletes play two or more sports.

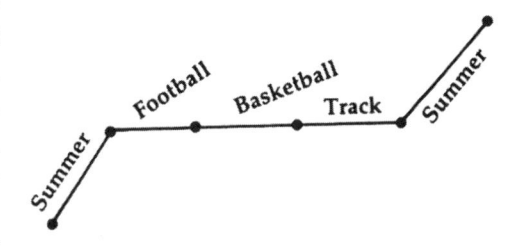

FIGURE 3.2 Deron's strength level.

High school sophomores may have a 250-pound (113-kilogram) squat, 175-pound (79-kilogram) bench, and a 160-pound (73-kilogram) clean. We don't want to maintain those lifts. To set up a maintenance program in high school is to set up a program of failure. The athletes will never reach their potential.

Mike's football coach did the BFS in-season program and followed the set–rep system. Gains achieved during the season were not as great as those that occurred in the off-season, but athletes made significant gains throughout each sport season (figure 3.3). Because the in-season program was the same for all sports, athletes could make smooth transitions from one sport season to the next. Mike stuck to his program faithfully all four years, broke an average of 400 personal records each year, and reached his potential. His lifts went off the chart!

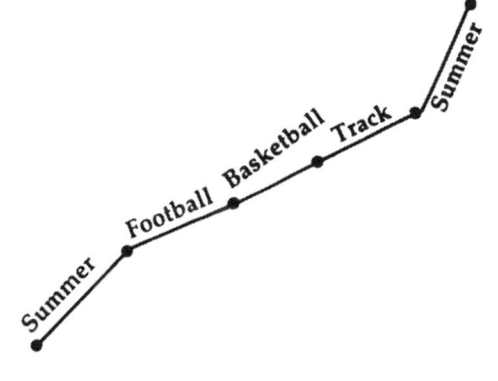

FIGURE 3.3 Mike's strength level.

Robin Jennings: An Insider's Look at Pro Baseball

Robin Jennings is in charge of BFS Baseball. His experience and knowledge of the game make him a valuable asset to the coaching staff, and his story provides a great example of the importance of strength and conditioning to reach the highest levels in sport.

When you consider how many millions of kids play baseball in the United States, the chances of being one of the 750 professional athletes in the big leagues are astronomically slim. Robin Jennings is one of those amazing athletes who defied the odds, playing professionally for 12 years and making it to the major leagues with Cincinnati, Chicago, Colorado, and Oakland. When Jennings told BFS that he was willing to let us interview him, we were ready with our questions.

Robin Jennings played professional baseball for 12 years and is currently the president of BFS baseball. He believes continuous strength training is coming to the forefront in baseball.

Born in Singapore in 1972, Jennings had early successes in high school, achieving his goals of being an all-conference, all-region, all-state, and all-metropolitan athlete. He signed a full athletic scholarship to Florida State University after two years at Manatee Junior College, but eventually he decided to sign professionally instead. On April 19, 1996, when he was 24 years old, he got called up to the big leagues by the Chicago Cubs. Now he is devoting his life to coaching so he can share his knowledge with young players.

In this exclusive interview, Robin opens up about the realities of the sport, from the steroid controversy to how the game is changing in the areas of strength and conditioning.

BFS: Looking back at your career, if you could do something differently, what would it be?

Jennings: I would have trained smarter in the areas of flexibility, strength training, and recovery. I was always dedicated to training, but I did some things the wrong way that resulted in harmful stress to my body. If you were to talk to some of the players and coaches I've worked with, they would say that I was injury prone. At the time, I just felt like I played the game hard and got hurt playing—now I know better.

BFS: Are kids who want to play pro baseball getting the right sort of guidance?

Jennings: On one hand, I believe there is enough information out there right now about how young people should train for baseball—that is, doing things that are fundamentally sound for their particular level. But too many kids are already worrying about what the

BFS: pros are doing. I'd like to see young people get back to the fundamentals and a foundation in strength.

BFS: What is your general philosophy about achieving success in baseball?

Jennings: This is going to sound very ordinary, but baseball is a repetitious, monotonous sport, and working on the fundamentals is what it takes to get better. It's all about muscle memory and repetition.

BFS: In the past, many baseball players thought there would be too much stress on the body if they did strength training during the season, especially on the road. What is the current thinking in this area?

Jennings: It's still divided. There are coaches at the professional level who encourage their players to make the effort to weight train on the road, and there's definitely a group that doesn't believe it's necessary for baseball.

BFS: What is your take on the steroid controversy?

Jennings: One of the most common misconceptions about the steroid controversy is thinking that it allows people who ordinarily wouldn't be able to hit home runs to hit home runs. Actually, guys who can hit the ball 500 feet (152 meters) with steroids could already hit the ball 400 feet (122 meters) without steroids. It's a matter of degree. Players who take performance-enhancing drugs are looking for an edge.

BFS: But do steroid users have longer careers than those who don't use steroids?

Jennings: I don't believe so. One of the major drawbacks of steroid use is that it can easily shorten your career because the injuries will eventually take over, not to mention the long-term effects the steroids have on your health.

BFS: Are chronic injuries common among pro baseball players?

Jennings: Almost every player will tell you that he's ailing in some fashion during the season almost every day. That's because you don't have the recovery time in baseball that you have in some other sports, even though it's not as physical. That's why strength training is really coming to the forefront in baseball, and coaches are trying to figure out what works and what doesn't.

BFS: How can baseball players overcome slumps?

Jennings: I believe a slump is a breakdown of the confidence you normally have about your natural ability. It's almost never a physical problem, but some athletes try to deal with it as if it were because

> *continued*

> continued

it's a lot easier to attack things from a physical perspective. The best book that I ever read dealing with sport psychology was a book my agent recommended to me: *The Inner Game of Tennis.* The book has to do with success and failure and how to deal with the mental side of sports. It just so happens to be a book about tennis, but the concepts directly relate to what is happening in baseball.

BFS: What do pro baseball players think about their fans?

Jennings: I think most players understand that without the fans they wouldn't have a job, so I hope that most of them keep that at the forefront and treat their fans with respect. Do I think some fans go to excess? Yes. When you walk out of the hotel to get some breakfast and the fans insist you sign all sorts of stuff, it can be annoying.

BFS: What is your opinion of Michael Jordan's attempt to play professional baseball? Did he give up on baseball too soon?

Jennings: I saw Michael play in a number of games. He's probably the greatest athlete of our generation, but his abilities in basketball just didn't translate into exceptional skills in baseball. Besides, it was late in his athletic career when he took up the game. The athletes who can go from one sport to another are truly amazing, because once you get to that level, all the skills are so sport specific. Deion Sanders, a prime example, was impressive, and Bo Jackson was one of the most phenomenal all-around athletes ever. But that's two guys in how long?

BFS: At the high school level, do you think it's better to play multiple sports?

Jennings: It's up to the individual, but I think playing multiple sports when you are young makes you a better athlete. I loved basketball and track, so I ended up doing those sports in high school and actually played football in my senior year. The time to concentrate on one sport is when you get feedback from an unbiased source that says you might go to the next level. That being said, you need to be realistic; 96 percent of all high school athletes will never play past high school.

BFS: Do you think athletes can burn out if they focus on one sport too early?

Jennings: Absolutely, and you have to think about what you could be missing. You know, one of my biggest regrets in life has nothing to do with sports—it was stopping playing an instrument in sixth grade. I'm 34 years old now, and I wish more than anything that I could

BFS: What sort of goals do you think are important for kids?

Jennings: I've always tried hard to set goals for myself, but realistic ones I can attain. In my freshman year in high school, I set a goal to play varsity. I came from a school in Northern Virginia, where that was a hard goal. I achieved that goal and then set higher goals.

I think that some kids, as well as some coaches and parents, forget that a lot of confidence comes from achieving incremental goals. Instead of setting a goal to play in the major leagues, a kid should start by focusing on making the Little League all-star team, then on making the high school baseball team, then on being a starter. Set and achieve goals one at a time, and eventually you may be prepared for playing in the big leagues.

CHAPTER 4

BFS Readiness Program

The Bigger Faster Stronger (BFS) readiness program has been designed for those who are not yet ready to engage in weight training programs performed by more physically mature athletes. After athletes go through the BFS readiness program, they will graduate to the BFS set–rep system. This chapter provides athletes and coaches with a program outlining where to start, how to perform the exercises, how to progress, how to coordinate other athletic activities into a total program, and how to graduate to the BFS set–rep system.

WHO SHOULD USE THE BFS READINESS PROGRAM?

Although many athletes will be ready to jump right into the BFS set–rep system, others are more suited to starting with the BFS readiness program. Here are some examples.

- **Middle school male and female athletes.** Most athletes or physical education students in the seventh grade should begin with the BFS readiness program. Some orthopedic surgeons believe that adolescents of this age are too young to start any kind of weight training, but the research proves otherwise, and we believe that the benefits outweigh the potential risks.

The BFS readiness program prepares young athletes for the BFS program by using light weights to teach perfect technique.

Without weight training, few young people can reach their athletic potential. One of the major concerns about weight training for young athletes is that it could damage the epiphyseal (growth) plates. Although injury to the epiphyseal plates may cause bone deformity, the risk that this will occur with weight training is no greater than it is with most sports. As for the risk that weight training will stunt growth, premature closing of the epiphyseal plates is related primarily to hormonal influences, not injury. Mel Siff, an exercise scientist whose doctoral thesis examined the biomechanics of soft tissues, addressed this subject.

"It has never been shown scientifically or clinically that the periodic imposition of large forces by weight training on the growing body causes damage to the epiphyseal plates," Siff says in his book *Facts and Fallacies of Fitness* (1998). "It is extremely misleading to focus on the alleged risks of weight training on children when biomechanical research shows that simple daily activities such as running, jumping, striking, or catching can impose far greater forces on the musculoskeletal system than very heavy weight training."

Siff also notes that bone density scans have proven that young people who do competitive weightlifting (i.e., the snatch and the clean and jerk) have higher bone densities than children who do not use weights, and clinical research has not shown any correlation between weight training and epiphyseal damage. Siff's comments are supported by an extensive Russian study on young athletes, published in a book titled *School of Height,* which concluded that heavy lifting tends to stimulate bone growth in young athletes rather than inhibit it.

Risk of injury is another area of concern for coaches and parents. Many studies have measured the rate of injuries associated with weight training compared with the injury rate in other sports. For example, a study published in 2001 in the *Journal of American Academy of Orthopaedic Surgeons* cited research showing that in children aged 5 to 14 years, the number of injuries from bicycling was almost 400 percent greater than the number of injuries from weightlifting.

In a review paper on resistance training for prepubescent and adolescents published in 2002 in *Strength and Conditioning Coach,* author Mark Shillington reported that only 0.7 percent (or 1,576) of sport-related injuries in school-aged children were caused by resistance training, compared with 19 percent caused by football and 15 percent caused by baseball. Dr. Mel Hayashi, a noted orthopedic surgeon, states, "The BFS readiness program should provide great benefits to the junior high athlete. I have no concerns as long as the athlete has good technique." Dr. Hayashi has been a chief orthopedic surgeon at the Olympic Games and is a former chief resident at the Mayo Clinic.

The truth is that weight training and competitive lifting are among the safest activities an athlete can participate in. For example, renowned Russian sport scientist Vladimir Zatsiorsky in his textbook *Science and Practice of Strength Training* (1995) had this to say about the dangers of weight training: "The risk of injury from a well-coached strength training program has been estimated to be about one per 10,000 athlete-exposures," with an athlete-exposure being defined as one athlete taking part in one training session or competition. "Compared to tackle football, alpine skiing, baseball pitching, and even sprint running, strength training is almost free of risk."

The success and popularity of BFS clinics are proof of the merits of early weight training. As young athletes strive to achieve the highest levels in competitive sport, they must participate in serious training at a younger age than the champions of the past did. This commitment is the price of success. Athletes are starting competitive sports at a younger age, including contact sports such as football, and as such they are subjecting their bodies to higher levels of stress than ever before. If young bodies are to handle the stress of this training, weight training is essential.

Many strength coaches at major universities throughout the United States have been asked when athletes should start weight training. The vast majority responded, "In junior high." In addition, the countries of the former Eastern Bloc start weight training at age 12.

Weight training is also one of the best ways to build self-confidence. A 7th grader can receive just as much satisfaction by going from 85 to 100 pounds (39-45 kilograms) on the bench press as a 12th grader can by going from 285 to 300 pounds (129-136 kilograms). Of course, strict supervision and proper technique are essential to making the BFS readiness program work in middle school.

- **High school female athletes.** Some girls go straight into the weight room and lift with the guys—they are not intimidated. Even though they use less weight, they can match the boys set for set and rep for rep. Our experience, however, tells us that many high school females would be better served by starting their weight training with the BFS readiness program. This is because fewer girls have a background in sport at a young age compared with boys, and they have not been introduced to the basics of sprinting and jumping.
- **High school male athletes.** If a male athlete cannot squat 145 pounds (66 kilograms) to parallel for 10 reps with good form, then we believe it's best to start with the BFS readiness program. At the beginning of the year, this program may include as many as 50 percent of 9th graders, 10 to 20 percent of 10th graders, and 5 percent of 11th and 12th graders.
- **Injured athletes.** Injured athletes may find the BFS readiness program to be of great benefit as they rehabilitate. We've found that athletes who have been involved with the BFS program tend to recover faster from injuries than those who did not use the BFS program or those who used other programs. The BFS readiness program uses higher reps and only two sets. Also, the strict attention to technique, which is made easier because lighter weights are used and fatigue does not become a factor, makes this an ideal program for any rehabilitating athlete.
- **Parents.** Many parents will find the BFS readiness program a great way to get started on a weight training program. They gain the added benefit of progressing on the same program that their sons or daughters are using.

BFS READINESS IN MIDDLE SCHOOL

The BFS readiness program can produce spectacular results in middle school. The program can be implemented in a physical education class in conjunction with other activities or as a separate entity. Parents and coaches are often surprised to discover how fast seventh graders can learn and profit from this program.

- **Weight training.** Coaches can teach the technique of the BFS core lifts with just the 45-pound (20-kilogram) barbell. A cycle of two or three days per week may be used, although generally two workouts per week is best, especially in the beginning. Doing three core lifts in a 40-minute physical education class is easy. On the first day, do box squats, towel benches, and power cleans. On the second day, do parallel squats, bench presses, and straight-leg deadlifts. If you have enough time, do auxiliary exercises.

The unique aspect of the BFS readiness program is its criteria for increasing poundage. Most programs allow athletes to increase weight when they do the last set successfully. In our program, they must not only do the prescribed number of sets and reps successfully but also do each set and rep with perfect technique. "A victory is a victory!" is not a motto that applies in the weight room. If a lift is performed with poor technique, such as not going to parallel in the squat, the repetition should not count. When the technique of the correct number of sets and reps has been judged perfect, the athlete may increase the weight by 5 pounds (2 kilograms) for the workout the following week. This system is amazing for producing great technique early on.

Graduation from the BFS readiness program occurs when a boy can parallel squat 145 pounds (66 kilograms) for two sets of 10 reps and bench-press 105 pounds (48 kilograms) or 90 percent of body weight (whichever is less) for two sets of 10 reps (see figure 4.1 on p. 42). If you really get after it, about one out of five students will graduate by the end of the seventh grade. After graduation, the athlete uses the standard BFS program. If the emphasis continues throughout the middle school years, many boys will be able to bench-press 200 pounds (91 kilograms), parallel squat 300 pounds (136 kilograms), and power clean 175 pounds (79 kilograms) before they enter high school.

- **Flexibility.** When I coached my son's eighth-grade football team, the whole team did the 9.5-minute BFS 1-2-3-4 flexibility program (covered in chapter 14). The parents knew that the players were expected to do flexibility exercises every day, and most of the kids did it on their own every day at home. All I had to do was teach the exercises and occasionally check on the players. If kids are given a chance to reach their upper limits, it's amazing how many will respond.

- **Agility.** My son's team also did the BFS dot drill (see chapter 11) every day on their own. My son did it in 47 seconds, and most of the 31 players did it in less than 60 seconds. Seeing a 13-year-old whip through the BFS dot drill in 50 seconds is impressive.

- **Speed and plyometrics.** Kids at any age can learn how to run correctly (see chapter 13). Want an edge? Teach seventh graders how to run: Less than 1 percent of U.S. seventh graders have had this seemingly basic instruction.

Teaching kids how to jump is also vital (see chapter 12). My son Matt helped me demonstrate plyometrics at a clinic I gave in Georgia. The high school senior basketball players were amazed when Matt jumped from a 20-inch (51-centimeter) box down to the floor, up to another 20-inch box, then another 20-inch box, and finally hopped up to a 38-inch (97-centimeter) desk. I was even surprised. Matt said, "Dad, that's nothing." The seniors were reluctant to try until a 13-year-old showed them how.

Questions and Answers

Many elementary schools use the BFS program. Following are some frequently asked questions regarding younger children.

1. **When can we start the BFS flexibility program?** I taught one of my daughters our flexibility program when she was in third grade. She mastered it in 15 minutes and began teaching the neighborhood kids. The BFS flexibility program can certainly be taught to all athletes in middle school.

2. **Wouldn't it be advantageous to have every athlete come into high school with great flexibility and with the daily habit of performing a 10-minute flexibility session?** Flexibility means injury prevention, which means speed, because injured athletes often cannot perform at their highest level. In the United States, no one does flexibility training at early ages. Any coach who can influence the right people to install the BFS flexibility program in middle school and grade school will have an edge, in addition to providing a great service.

3. **When can we start plyometrics?** In the United States, we generally do not teach athletes at any level how to jump. All we do when we test an athlete on a vertical jump is say, "Jump as high as you can!" Athletes must master specific techniques to reach their maximum. We can and should teach grade school and middle school athletes the techniques of the vertical jump and the standing long jump. As for plyometrics, there is no reason why we cannot incorporate basic plyometric drills in the total middle school conditioning program. Two 10-minute plyometric sessions per week can pay big dividends by the time those athletes enter the high school program.

4. **When can we start teaching the BFS sprint technique?** The longer athletes are allowed to run incorrectly, the harder it will be for them to unlearn bad habits and learn correct technique. As I worked with NBA hopefuls at tryout camp for the Utah Jazz and with players for the Sacramento Kings, I asked them about their previous work with flexibility, plyometrics, and sprint training. It was zilch. Zero! NBA players usually have poor flexibility. I asked them if they wanted greater flexibility and if they would have liked to learn how to run at an early age. Of course, they all said yes.

5. **How is the BFS readiness program different from the high school program?** There is little difference. The seventh grader can perform the same flexibility program, the same agility drills, the same beginning plyometrics, and the same sprint system. The only real difference is in the lifting program, although both programs use the same core lifts and the same concept in selecting auxiliary exercises.

6. **What results can we expect from the BFS readiness program?** When coaches who seek excellence choose the BFS readiness program, their athletes will accomplish great things. A high school with an enrollment of 1,000 can expect 25 athletes to come from the middle school each year with these abilities: a minimum 300-pound (136-kilogram) parallel squat with great form, a minimum 200-pound (91-kilogram) bench press, and a minimum 175-pound (79-kilogram) clean and press with great form. These players will also possess great flexibility, good plyometric ability, and correct running form. With these abilities come great side benefits, such as increased self-confidence, good work habits, and a winning attitude.

BFS READINESS: WEIGHT TRAINING

To minimize the risk of injury from any conditioning program, coaches must teach proper technique. During BFS clinics, our clinicians not only teach athletes how to lift and spot properly but also instruct coaches how to teach the proper lifting and spotting techniques. As the proverb goes, "Give a man a fish and you feed him for a day. Teach a man to fish and you feed him for a lifetime." With that in mind, here are the details of the BFS readiness weight training program.

Getting Started

Start with just the 45-pound (20-kilogram) Olympic bar on each core lift, although for some athletes (especially girls), a lighter, 15-pound (7-kilogram) technique bar may be necessary. Do not worry if this amount of weight is light and does not seem challenging. We are going to test for two things: First, can they perform two sets of 5 or 10 reps, and second, can they perform each rep and each set with great technique? Focus on perfect technique—athletes will have plenty of time to become stronger later in their athletic career.

Therefore, if 45 pounds (20 kilograms) is too heavy (which might be the case on the hang clean or the bench press), start with less. Don't worry if you have to start with less—it doesn't matter where you start, only where you finish!

Progressing

Two things must happen before progressing to greater weight. Athletes must be able to complete two sets of 10 or 5 reps, and they must be able to do each rep of each set with perfect technique. When they can do these two things, they may go up 5 pounds (2 kilograms) the next week on the same lift.

Be sure to record the date of the workout (see figure 4.1). All serious athletes keep weight training records. Athletes will have pride and satisfaction as they work up in poundage toward graduation. If they cannot do the two sets of 10 or 5 reps with perfect technique, they must keep repeating the same weight until they can.

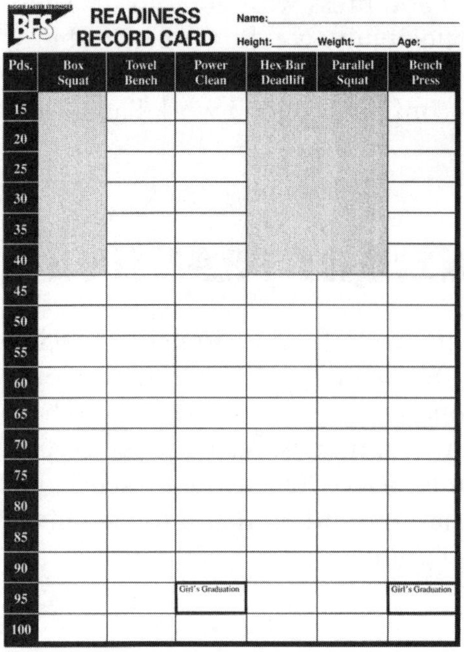
READINESS RECORD CARD

Name:

Height: Weight: Age:

Pds.	Box Squat	Towel Bench	Power Clean	Hex-Bar Deadlift	Parallel Squat	Bench Press
15						
20						
25						
30						
35						
40						
45						
50						
55						
60						
65						
70						
75						
80						
85						
90						
95			Girl's Graduation			Girl's Graduation
100						

FIGURE 4.1 BFS readiness record card.

Judging Technique

A coach, parent, or training partner should judge an athlete's technique. When athletes train alone, obviously they will have to judge themselves. Everyone should train with a partner for three reasons: The partner can motivate the lifter, spot the lifter, and judge the lifter's technique.

There are three judging rules for each lift. If lifters break any of the rules during any set, they may not progress the next week.

Bench Press and Towel Bench Press

Athletes should perform two sets of 10 reps each. Use these judging criteria:

- **Touching the chest.** If the bar doesn't touch the chest or towel, it doesn't count.
- **Even extension.** One arm should not go up way before the other arm, but a little disparity is acceptable because individual athletes may have structural differences that slightly affect technique. Also, look for uneven elbows at the bottom position. Sometimes one elbow is tucked into the chest while the other is out to the side—don't count it! Force the athlete to do it right.
- **Hips down.** By using a wide stance, with the feet underneath and shoulders forced toward the hips, athletes will be less likely to excessively arch and lift their hips from the bench. All lifters, especially young lifters, should observe this rule because it will give them better chest development.

Box Squat

Athletes should perform two sets of 10 reps each. Use these judging criteria:

- **Arched lower back.** The lower back must be locked in, not rounded.
- **Pause on the box.** The athlete must sit on the box, keeping the back locked in, and rock back slightly before driving forward and up. If the athlete just touches the box and comes up, the lift doesn't count.
- **Finish the lift.** At the finish of the lift, the athlete must come up on the toes to better simulate the action that occurs in jumping.

Squat

Athletes should perform two sets of 10 reps each. Use these judging criteria:

- **Arched lower back.** The lower back must be locked in, not rounded.

- **Squat depth.** The athlete must squat down until the tops of the thighs are at least parallel with the floor. Many beginning lifters will find this difficult.
- **Stance.** The stance should look like an athlete's stance, not narrow or wide. Watch the toes—a 45-degree angle is too much. Also, watch the knees. If they come too far in on the way up (a little inward rotation is natural), do not count the lift.

Power Clean

Athletes should perform two sets of five reps each. Use these judging criteria:
- **Arched lower back.** In the starting position, the lower back should be locked in.
- **Acceleration.** The athlete should pull the bar off the floor slowly and then jump with the bar close to the body. Elbows should be high, with the chin away from the chest.
- **Catch position.** The athlete must rack the bar to deltoids properly and be in an athletic position. Racking the barbell properly involves resting the bar on the shoulders with the elbows high and the hands relaxed to reduce the stress on the wrists and elbows.

Straight-Leg Deadlift

Athletes should perform two sets of 10 reps each. This is primarily a stretching exercise and as such heavy weights are not used. Use these judging criteria:
- **Speed.** The athlete should perform the lift slowly and with control.
- **Weight selection.** Don't use heavy weights—the maximum weight should be 55 pounds (25 kilograms).

Organization

The BFS readiness program takes only 45 minutes two times per week. A maximum of five athletes should use one barbell, allowing one to lift, three to spot, and one to get ready. The athletes should rotate in order. If the program is part of a physical education class, the class could be divided into three groups, with the groups rotating every 15 minutes. For example, group 1 does core lifts, group 2 does auxiliary lifts, and group 3 does agility and running skills. The equipment needed to conduct this program for 15 athletes is as follows.

Approximate cost:

Olympic bench press	$350
Squat rack	$500
Squat box	$80
Three 300 lb (136 kg) Olympic sets	$1,000
Training plates	$70
	$2,000

The cost goes up about $150 for each additional group of five athletes. The equipment suggestions are for heavy-duty equipment meant for years of constant use. Equipment for home use would be less expensive.

Graduation

Graduation depends on performance, not age. Some children mature faster than others do, and some learn technique faster. Graduation requirements favor the bigger and heavier athletes to some extent, so coaches should make a judgment call as to when some lighter athletes are ready to move to the next level of the program. You will see in table 4.1 that a male athlete must do two sets of 10 reps with 145 pounds (66 kilograms) on the squat, and a female must do 105 pounds (48 kilograms). Everyone starts with 45 pounds (20 kilograms) and goes up at a maximum rate of 5 pounds (2 kilograms) a week.

Graduation requirements are based on three lifts: the squat, bench, and hang clean. These are basic core lifts that should be used throughout an athlete's career. An athlete must pass all three lifts to graduate (see table 4.1). Although they are important lifts, the box squat, towel bench, and straight-leg deadlifts are not included in graduation requirements.

Table 4.1 Graduation Requirements

Event	Male	Female
Squat (2 sets of 10 reps)	145 lb	105 lb
Bench (2 sets of 10 reps)	105 lb or 90% of body weight	75 lb or 90% of body weight
Power clean (2 sets of 5 reps)	105 lb or 90% of body weight	75 lb or 90% of body weight

Graduation means that the athlete is ready to begin the regular BFS program, a more strenuous program requiring a more mature frame. The total BFS program allows all athletes to reach their potential soon enough.

Giving awards for graduation from the BFS readiness program will make graduation special and develop pride of accomplishment. Awards might be ribbons, medals, shirts, or simply placing the athletes' names on a chart. Give an award for each event passed.

PART II

Strength Exercises

CHAPTER 5

Six Absolutes of Perfect Technique

Bigger Faster Stronger (BFS) has developed six training principles, or absolutes, that are amazingly effective in teaching perfect technique not only in the weight room but also in any sport. Coaches who learn the six BFS absolutes can dramatically elevate their athletes' strength and their own coaching ability.

Without keeping you in suspense, here are the six absolutes of perfect technique:

1. Eyes on target.
2. Use an athletic or jump stance.
3. Be tall.
4. Spread the chest (lock in the lower back).
5. Align the toes.
6. Align the knees (knees over toes).

One reason the six absolutes are so effective is that they encourage all coaches to use the same terminology when teaching weight training and sport skills. After all, how can athletes be expected to follow instructions exactly when the instructions they receive vary from coach to coach? Such confusion also goes against the concept of developing a unified program. When teaching the squat, instead of one coach saying "Make your chest big" and another coach at batting practice saying "Spread the chest," both coaches will simply use say, "Spread the chest."

EYES ON TARGET

The eyes-on-target absolute is a useful tool in sports such as football. For example, it is late in the game and you are behind. You're on defense and you must create a turnover. Instead of tackling with your eyes on the ball carrier's chest, you could try targeting the ball. At BFS clinics, athletes learn this absolute so thoroughly that by the end of the day all you have to do is say, "Eyes!" and an immediate correction takes place. Figures 5.1*a* and *b* illustrate examples of eyes on target.

Eyes on target is a great tool to use in the weight room, especially in squats. When an athlete looks up at the ceiling while beginning the squatting movement at the top position, everything might seem comfortable and right. At the bottom position is when things go bad. It is virtually impossible to look at the same point on the ceiling in the bottom position. The eyes move, the head moves, and the body moves out of position. Don't look down at the ground; this can be as dangerous as tackling a ball carrier with the head down (in figure skating, a common expression is, "Look at the ice, fall on the ice!"). Don't look up and don't look down, but stare intensely straight ahead and fix your eyes on a single point throughout the entire lift.

Eyes on target is one of the great secrets that will give you a big edge on your opponents. Use it often.

FIGURE 5.1 Perfect stretch position *(a)* and hex-bar deadlift *(b)* position with the eyes on target.

USE AN ATHLETIC OR JUMP STANCE

When talking about stances, many coaches talk about positioning the feet about shoulder width apart, or narrower than hip width. That phrasing will no longer be acceptable, because coaches will make certain that everything in the program is relevant to athletics.

All sports require the same two basic stances—the jump stance and the athletic stance. We use the jump stance primarily when we lift from the floor with lifts such as the power clean, power snatch, and hex-bar deadlift because the force from the legs is directed in a vertical line to produce maximum power. We use an athletic stance with lifts such as the squat or the rack position in the power clean (when the bar is caught on the shoulders). This is because the wider foot stance and the lower center of gravity associated with the athletic stance are more stable.

All sports use basically the same stance. It doesn't matter if it's tennis, softball, or a ready position in football; the stance is the same. It is imperative to always squat from an athletic stance so we can groove the strength and power we build from that stance. We want these gains to be meaningful and functional.

At clinics, our clinicians say they are a shortstop or linebacker and then they get into various stances: narrow, wide, toes out, and just right. From that perspective, every athlete and coach can immediately determine a good stance from a goofy stance. This is the athletic stance. Next, the clinicians ask the athletes and coaches to look at their feet as they step up to a line to do a standing long jump. Again, they get into various stances. It is easy to distinguish a jump stance from the others because you look like an athlete who is ready to either hit or jump. You are in either an athletic position or a jump position, an athletic stance or jump stance.

Let's take a closer look at how this absolute works in squatting. In squatting, there are three basic squatting stances: bodybuilding, powerlifting, and athletic.

- **Bodybuilding stance.** Bodybuilders generally use a narrow stance, often with the toes straight ahead and sometimes with a board placed underneath the heels. This method is used to develop the teardrop-shaped muscle of the lower thigh called the *vastus medialis*. Because this style places high shearing forces on the knee (i.e., forces trying to pry the joint apart), it should generally be avoided by athletes.

- **Powerlifting stance.** Many powerlifters use a wide stance with the toes flared out, or a powerlifting stance. Some powerlifters use a narrow stance, with the toes pointed forward quite a lot, and there are a few powerlifters who use an athletic stance. Powerlifters use whatever stance allows them to squat the most weight, even though some of these techniques significantly increase the risk of knee and hip injuries. Other athletes, however, should be more concerned about becoming stronger and more powerful with minimal risk of injury.

- **Athletic stance.** When discussing squatting stances, invariably the experts say, "Take about a shoulder-width stance." This is meant to be an athletic stance, but is there a better way to explain it? Yes!

Ask basketball players to get in a rebounding stance and baseball players to look like a shortstop. Tell football players to get in a linebacker stance and volleyball and tennis players to assume their ready position. At clinics, we get into a bodybuilder's squatting stance and ask, "Does this look like a linebacker?" The kids say, "No." Then we get into a wide powerlifting stance with the toes flared way out and ask, "How about this position? Does this look like a football, basketball, or baseball player?" Everyone always laughs. Then we get into an athletic stance, and it's amazing because you'll see that the ready position for all mainstream high school sports is essentially the same.

As athletes and coaches spot each other, they should make certain lifters look like authentic athletes at all times with their stances. Jump from a jump stance, and build your power and strength from an athletic

FIGURE 5.2 Athletic stance *(a)* and jump stance *(b)*.

stance. Because the terminology is more precise, calling for an athletic stance is a far superior terminology than saying to position your feet about shoulder width apart. This terminology also sends a message that we are athletes and ensures that the squatting stance remains the same when making a transition from basketball to baseball or from volleyball to softball (see figures 5.2*a* and *b*). Regardless of whether the most appropriate stance is an athletic or jump stance, having the same basic terminology will help make coaching more precise and uniform for all sport teams.

BE TALL

You need to be tall all the time, whether you're sitting, walking, sprinting, lifting, or even stretching. You can't slump or lean forward outside your center of gravity and expect to perform well. Being tall produces dramatic improvements in posture, improvements that will translate into better sport performance and reduced risk of injury.

Here's a simple test to determine if you're standing tall. Stand with your heels, buttocks, back, shoulders, and head against a wall. Now try to slide one hand behind your lower back, at belly-button level or where there is the greatest arch in your back. If you are standing tall, the thickest part of the hand will just fill the gap between the wall and the back. If the hand slides right through or gets stuck, you are not standing tall.

Coaches can determine whether athletes are standing tall simply by observing their relaxed, standing posture. Look at each of them from the side and note the position of the shoulder and head. Does the head thrust forward? Are the knees locked and is the pelvis thrust forward? If the answer is yes to these questions, the athlete is not being tall.

Athletes who stand tall look like winners. When athletes are tall, their waist will appear flatter and their shoulders broader. The common reaction of friends toward athletes who learn to be tall is that they've lost weight! And in sports where there is an aesthetic component, such as diving, gymnastics, and figure skating, the postural improvements from being tall will be reflected in higher scores from the judges. Further, the postural improvements from being tall can help prevent the lower back problems and other injuries.

If an athlete is slouching, say, "Be tall!" Immediately, good things happen. If an athlete is bending at the waist with a rounded back, the quickest way to correct this problem is to say, "Be tall!" Fine-tuning comes with the other absolutes, especially keeping eyes on target and spreading the chest. All these terms are designed to help any athlete get into a correct and efficient alignment.

FIGURE 5.3 Poor squatting position (a) and good squatting position with the athlete lifting tall (b).

This absolute should be used with most lifts in the weight room. In squatting, every athlete needs to squat with the feeling of sitting tall. You do not want to bend over with the head down and hips high; this can injure the lower back and does not develop functional strength (see figures 5.3a and b). Outside the weight room, being tall should be used as often as possible. For example, after full speed is attained in sprinting, athletes should sprint tall. Another example would be throwing a discus or a ball; bending forward causes technique problems and inefficiency. Finally, when performing the hex-bar deadlift, for example, focusing on being tall throughout the entire lift helps ensure that the spine is in proper alignment and that the legs are properly used during the lift.

At BFS clinics, athletes thoroughly learn the absolute of being tall by the end of the day. Coaches in attendance use the six absolutes repeatedly. We always find it rewarding to see the rapid improvements in both coaches and athletes, especially with coaches who have no significant background in weight training. In just one day they become skilled in correcting technique flaws. Coaches should make certain their athletes are being tall in all they do.

SPREAD THE CHEST

This is a fantastic coaching secret that I accidentally discovered during a BFS clinic. I was frustrated because several boys could not lock in their lower back. I blurted out, "Spread the chest!" To my amazement, their lower backs immediately went from poor to great. We now say

"Spread the chest" to athletes when they deadlift or power clean. Once athletes experience the lower back locking into place as they spread the chest while sitting in a chair, they can usually have the same experience without the chair. Sitting in the chair just makes it a whole lot easier. Several years later, I noticed that some strength coaches were saying, "Make your chest big." It is the same principle, but we believe "Spread the chest" is a clearer coaching term.

Spreading the chest and locking in the lower back work together, but you must visualize and coach both techniques. The lower back must swoop into a concave position that exercise physiologists refer to as the neutral spine. When athletes spread their chests, the lower back will start to lock in properly in a concave position.

Matt Shepard is shown in figure 5.4a trying to hit a home run. Think he can do it? How about in figure 5.4b? Think he has a better chance in this position? Okay, then how do you fix the problem and help all athletes go from wherever they are now to a rating of 10? Simple! Use the six absolutes.

In a BFS clinic, one of the first things our clinicians do is bring down six athletes from the bleachers. They line up 2 yards (2 meters) apart and stand sideways to the audience. We then give the command "Hit," which means to pop to an athletic stance so that the athlete is in an athletic ready position. We grade their position on a scale of 1 to 10. From the sideways position, we are looking mostly at the lower back. Almost always there will be an athlete who looks like figure 5.4a. This

FIGURE 5.4 Poor batting stance, using a rounded back *(a)* and proper batting stance *(b)*.

A BFS clinician supervises the technique of athletes squatting during a clinic.

position is about a 3. It is not uncommon to give a rating of 1 or 2. Can you imagine squatting, jumping, tackling, or doing anything athletic from this position?

During a clinic, we ask all athletes and coaches sitting in the bleachers to get their feet into an athletic stance like the six athletes in front. Next, we say, "Be tall and spread the chest." Most athletes will improve dramatically. Our clinicians might have to make some slight adjustments by pulling back slightly on an athlete's shoulders or being more forceful in giving the command to spread the chest.

A few people will still have problems getting a kinesthetic feel for the correct position, and there are two coaching guidelines to help these athletes. First, we have them put their hands on their knees with some pressure, as in figure 5.5a. Most of those who can't get the kinesthetic feel will be successful from this position. Those who still cannot get into a correct position then sit on a bench or squat box as in figure 5.5b. Again we say, "Be tall and spread the chest." We might have to mold them by pushing in on their lower back and pulling back on their shoulders, but they should be able to do it.

From this sitting position, they squat up a few inches and see if they can stay in the correct position. Some will and some won't. For the ones who still have a problem, we simply start over. The last step is to stand

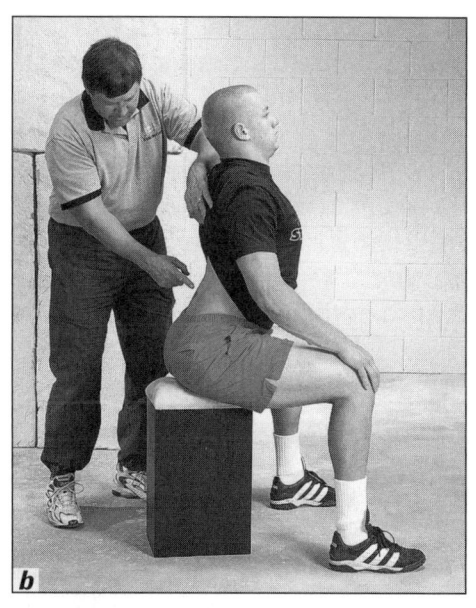

FIGURE 5.5 Getting the kinetic feel for proper alignment when standing *(a)* and sitting *(b)*.

erect. We tell them to try to remember the correct position and then do it. If they still can't, we start over on the box. Most of the time no one has to start over, even if we are working with 100 athletes.

The athletes and coaches at a BFS clinic will hear the expression "Spread the chest" several hundred times, and athletes will need to be corrected throughout the entire school year. It should just be part of everyone's vocabulary. Also, in the weight room it is every spotter's duty to make sure that whoever is lifting is lifting with perfect technique. If the lower back is even 1 percent from perfect, coaches and athletes should issue the command, "Be tall and spread the chest."

You can use this same BFS absolute in any activity: running, jumping, stretching, or sport practice. Athletes will be better if the lower back is correct. They will be less injury prone if the lower back is correct. And, all they have to do is spread the chest!

ALIGN THE TOES

This may sound strange, but athletes' toes should always be aligned. This means that the toes should either be straight ahead (jump stance) or slightly pointed out for balance (athletic stance).

In lifting, all coaches and athletes should be watching the toes as part of the six absolutes. Often athletes will point their toes out too far in the hex-bar deadlift stance and need to be corrected. Likewise, athletes sometimes point their toes way out on a squat to help them lift more weight. Fight this tendency by asking the question, "Is what we are doing going to help us win?" Is the objective to lift more weight, or win the athletic contest? The answer is obvious—we want to build strength we can use in the athletic arena.

A total strength and conditioning program involves, of course, a lot more than just lifting weights. It also involves stretching, jumping, and sprinting. The toes need to be aligned correctly in all of these phases of strength and conditioning. Here are some examples.

- **Sprinting.** The toes should point straight ahead with the eyes at 45 degrees (see figure 5.6). This is perfect. Often athletes point the toes out or look too far up. Coaches should correct this athlete's position by shouting, "Toes!" or "Eyes!"

- **Stretching.** Correct toe alignment in stretching is often neglected. Get the toes right in everything you do, every time you do it so that correct toe alignment becomes a habit. For example, in figure 5.7a the athlete is demonstrating one of the BFS stretches on the wall (back-leg stretch). Look at the back foot; the toes are pointed out. This is a common error that can be easily corrected. Figure 5.7b shows this stretch being done correctly.

FIGURE 5.6 Proper sprint start position.

Finally, look at figure 5.8a, which demonstrates poor toe alignment of the front foot in the hip flexor stretch. The toes should not be pointed out but should be straight, as shown in the correct position of figure 5.8b.

This technique tip is fairly well known, but it's still the cause of many mistakes for athletes. Most athletes point their toes out naturally for balance, but many times they point their toes out so far that their body weight is shifted primarily on their heels and outside of their feet (generally, more than 10 degrees from the midline of the body for each foot). No problem. Simply go back to the athletic stance formula. Ask the question, "Do you look like a linebacker, shortstop, or basketball player?" Remember, maximum power comes from an athletic stance that includes the toes only being pointed slightly out.

Six Absolutes of Perfect Technique 59

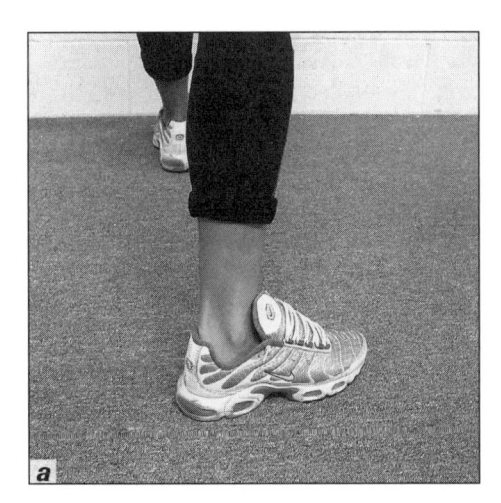

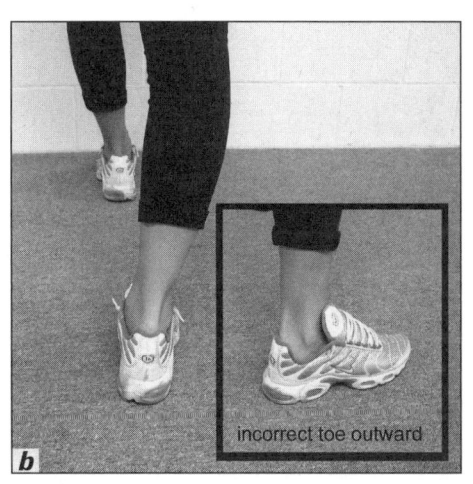

FIGURE 5.7 Toes improperly aligned in the back-leg stretch (a) and toes properly aligned, facing forward (b).

FIGURE 5.8 Hip flexor stretch with toes to the side in an improper alignment (a) and with toes aligned correctly (b).

It does not take long for an athlete to experience dramatic improvements in technique using the toes-aligned absolute. All athletes should act as assistant coaches and coach their teammates when spotting or performing any phase of strength and conditioning. If your goal is to win, then all athletes and coaches must be unified in helping each other become great.

ALIGN THE KNEES

The knees must be over the toes at all times in the weight room, in every phase of strength and conditioning, in every drill, and in every athletic movement.

Yelling "Knees!" is a cue to force the knees out over the toes. Take athletes and get them into a ready position and grade their knees on a scale of 1 to 10. There are always bad knees, and it is rare to give a 10 until this absolute has been coached.

Many times the knees will be way forward in front of the toes. The athlete needs to learn to balance on the entire foot; the heels cannot come up. Be tall, spread the chest, keep eyes on target, and sit with the hips well back. This will keep the knees aligned over the toes.

Knees that are in perfect alignment will be straight from every position. A good test is to take a ruler and place the top end at the middle of an athlete's knee. The bottom of the ruler should be at the middle of the athlete's toes. If the ruler is inside or outside, the position is incorrect. Sometimes, the knees will be outside the toes. This is almost always due to a narrow stance. Simply widen the stance to resolve this problem.

Sometimes beginning athletes squat with their knees too far forward and the heels off the ground. This posture puts too much pressure on the patella (kneecap) area, besides being absolutely ineffective. If the knees are past the tips of the toes, they are too far forward. To help correct this, use the partner system and practice squatting with the hips back and the knees vertical, as straight as possible. Another great way to learn how to balance is to try a front squat with a light weight. This will help athletes practice the art of stabilizing their body correctly.

Squatting with knees out puts unwanted pressure on the lateral collateral ligaments (located on the outside of the knee). The knees-out problem is easy to correct: Simply widen the stance until the knees are aligned directly over the toes.

The most common problem is that athletes let their knees come together (figure 5.9a), putting pressure on the medial collateral ligament (located on the inside of the knee). This is especially true with female athletes and middle school boys. The knees-in problem is more difficult to correct than the knees-out problem. The first step is to yell "Knees!" to athletes while they are squatting or doing some other lift. This is a signal to force the knees out over the toes (figure 5.9b). This signal may or may not work the first time. If it doesn't work, the second correction technique is to lightly tap the inside of the athlete's knee. This kinesthetic approach gives the athlete a feel for the problem. The cure usually happens after only a few light taps. If the problem persists, videotape the

FIGURE 5.9 Incorrect squat position with the knees in *(a)* and correct squat position with the knees over the toes *(b)*.

athletes so that they can see the problem. This combination of coaching guidelines will almost always do the trick.

You can use this coaching absolute for any activity. Athletes will perform better in all these areas if they keep their knees aligned—knees over toes. All you have to do is yell "Knees!" and positive things will happen.

Study these teaching points of the six BFS absolutes, write them down, post them in your weight room, memorize them, and watch the difference that they will make.

CHAPTER 6

Parallel Squat and Squat Variations

The parallel squat is the king of all exercises. If athletes do nothing but parallel squats, they will have a good program—not great, but good. Conversely, if they leave out the squats, minimize them, or perform them incorrectly, it won't matter what type of exercises they perform, what machines they use, or what training system they follow. Without the squat, athletes cannot fulfill their potential.

The parallel squat builds the foundation for speed, regardless of the athlete's size. A football player who is 6 feet, 4 inches (193 centimeters) tall; weighs 265 pounds (120 kilograms); and has good athletic ability can run a 40-yard (37-meter) dash in 4.6 seconds if he practices the squat. If that athlete does some other type of free-weight exercise or substitutes a machine for the squat, he will be lucky to run the same distance in 5.0 seconds.

Although most high school weight training programs include squats, many coaches allow their athletes to squat way too high. In an eight-team conference, probably four to five schools will squat high. Even the two or three schools whose athletes squat low enough will often have serious technique or spotting problems that decrease the effectiveness of the exercise and increase the risk of injury. You can make a quantum leap over your opponents by performing the parallel squat correctly.

BFS Vice President John Rowbotham teaches perfect squatting and spotting technique at a clinic he gave at Sickles High School in Tampa, Florida.

SQUATS, KNEES, AND INJURIES

Are squats bad for the knees? Despite evidence to the contrary, this question is continually raised, even by those who have no connection to athletics or physical education.

Much of the controversy originated from the belief that squats were harmful to the knees, an idea that was introduced by Dr. Karl K. Klein when he published the results of a study in 1961 that concluded that full squats could adversely affect knee stability. In the years that followed, flaws in the study were revealed and the results could not be reproduced. Further, peer-reviewed papers, such as one by Fleck and Falkel published in *Sports Medicine* in 1986, showed exactly opposite results—weightlifters and powerlifters tended to possess tighter knee joints than athletes in control groups and were less susceptible to knee injuries. Even though in his later writings Klein said he was not opposed to parallel squats, the damage had been done.

Over time, weightlifters, powerlifters, and sport scientists were able to convince the medical community and the public that squats are not harmful to the knees. One sport scientist who has written numerous peer-reviewed papers on the benefits of squats is Michael Stone. Stone and other researchers have found that performing squats by descending under complete control to achieve a parallel position results in many positive changes, including the following:

- The lower-body muscles become stronger and bigger, especially the quadriceps and hamstrings.
- The tendons become thicker and stronger.
- The knee ligaments become thicker and stronger.
- The entire articular capsule of the knee becomes thicker.
- The bones of the legs become stronger and slightly bigger because of increased capillarization.
- The cartilage of the knee becomes more resistant to injury.

These positive effects explain why athletes who do squats correctly have far fewer knee injuries than those who do not squat at all. Including squats and performing them properly is especially important for female athletes, because they are up to five times more likely to suffer knee injuries than male athletes are in sports such as basketball and volleyball. According to the American Orthopaedic Society for Sports Medicine (AOSSM), each year approximately 20,000 high school girls suffer serious knee injuries, most involving the anterior cruciate ligament (ACL), which helps stabilize the knee.

Proper squatting technique offers athletes the best defense against knee injuries. That being said, deep squats can present some danger to the knee joint, especially if the lifter comes down fast, is out of control, or bounces at the bottom position. Common sense tells us that an athlete who does deep squats with, say, 400 pounds (181 kilograms) is asking for problems if he comes down hard and bounces at the deep bottom position. But if an athlete lifting the same weight comes down under control to the parallel-squat position and then comes up, the knee joint should be in no danger whatsoever.

SQUAT DEPTH

Beyond injury prevention, squats are a key exercise for all athletes because just practicing the sport is not enough to reach the highest levels of athletic performance. For example, football linemen need to be big and strong, but simply playing football will do little to make athletes bigger and stronger. Baseball and softball players need to improve their muscle power to hit the ball far, but just practicing the swing will not do much to make these athletes more powerful. The squat is crucial because it strengthens the biggest and strongest muscles of the body. But if athletes aren't squatting to the proper depth, the gains are greatly reduced.

Understanding the importance of depth in squats is imperative. We base our standards on a parallel depth or slightly below it. The American high school standard is 500 pounds (227 kilograms) for males with heavy builds and 325 pounds (147 kilograms) for females with heavy builds. The all-state standard is 400 pounds (181 kilograms) for males and 235 pounds (107 kilograms) for females. Bigger Faster Stronger (BFS) set those standards to help athletes and coaches understand when an athlete achieves something unique. Only a special athlete with a thorough understanding of how to do squats can reach those standards. If an athlete squats a foot (30 centimeters) or 3 inches (8 centimeters) too high with 500 pounds (227 kilograms), it is meaningless. Not a whole lot is really happening, and the athlete will miss out on great benefits.

The guiding principle in squatting is that it's necessary to squat so that the tops of the upper thighs are at least horizontal to the floor and the hamstrings are strongly activated. The hamstrings (rear thigh muscles) are a key muscle in sprinting. If athletes don't squat low enough, they only activate the quadriceps (front thigh muscles). Further, if they do not squat low enough, then they will not improve knee stability, and they may even decrease knee stability by creating muscle imbalances.

At BFS, we offer a simple test to help athletes and coaches determine the proper depth—the marble test. If athletes were to place an imaginary marble (or dowel) on the middle of the top of the thighs during their deepest squat position, which way would the marble roll? If the marble would roll toward the knees, the athlete is not squatting low enough. If the marble would stay stationary or roll toward the hips, the depth is fine. What you'll find by using this standard is that the bottom of the thighs must be below parallel at the bottom of the squat. The marble test is better than judging the position of the bottom of the thigh because athletes with large legs must squat considerably lower using the marble test.

Does BFS have a problem with athletes squatting lower than parallel? Certainly not. All we are saying is that an athlete must squat to at least parallel to effectively work the hamstrings. As for the sport of powerlifting, the extraordinarily heavy weight lifted by many powerlifters suggests that there has been considerable leniency among some organizations as to what parallel is. Additionally, supportive gear can often add hundreds of pounds to a powerlifter's best result, and the extremely wide stance used by many powerlifters is not the athletic stance that BFS believes to have the best carryover to athletics. Powerlifters are trying to lift the heaviest weight possible over the shortest distance possible, whereas at BFS we are trying to lift in such a manner as to have the best carryover to athletics.

If Olympic weightlifters squat all the way down, and in competition they actually bounce out of the bottom position, why doesn't BFS recommend this style? After all, knee injuries to competitive weightlifters are rare, especially compared with other sports. What is wrong with going all the way down?

If athletes have a qualified Olympic lifting coach to work with them on this squatting method and the coach believes this form of squatting is superior, fine. But the reality is that a coach in high school may have 50 kids to work with at the same time, and it is difficult for strength coaches to give the one-on-one attention this type of squatting deserves. Additionally, there are relatively few qualified Olympic lifting coaches in the United States.

Squatting deep places the lower back at a higher risk of injury because the compression forces on the spine become greater as the athlete leans forward into the bottom position. Unless athletes have exceptional flexibility and proper supervision, their lower back will round when they squat all the way down. Rounding places a great deal of unnatural stress on the lower vertebrae of the back (L3, L4, and L5). This stress is compounded by the fact that the compression forces on the spine have been estimated to be six times greater at the bottom of a full squat than at the top (e.g., an athlete squatting 200 pounds [91 kilograms] would have 1,200 pounds [544 kilograms] of compression forces at the bottom). Again, unless an athlete has exceptional flexibility and one-on-one coaching from a qualified Olympic lifting coach, it would be better to go with a parallel squat or slightly below.

Finally, there is the argument that squatting all the way down doesn't work the quads and hamstrings through the full range of motion. That's true, but that's why BFS has glute–ham raises and lunges as high priority auxiliary exercises. Both of these exercises put minimal stress on the lower back while working the quads, especially the inner thigh muscle called the *vastus medialis* (which crosses the knee joint and therefore is key to maintaining knee stability) and all four heads of the hamstrings.

PRESQUAT TECHNIQUE

- **Equipment.** Before squatting, you must have the proper equipment. It's best to squat inside a power rack, with safety pins adjusted to the proper height. However, the safety pins should be thought of as death control, or a last-resort method of ensuring the athlete's safety, because dropping any barbell on these pins from more than a few inches can easily damage the barbell. Also, it's better to use Olympic barbells that have center knurling in order to properly secure the weight on the shoulders, as well as a stiffer barbell. The more flexible (and more expensive) Olympic bars are great for power cleans, but that same flexibility makes it difficult to control the barbell during a squat.

When you are ready to squat, you must make several important technique preparations—getting a secure grip, properly positioning the bar on the shoulders, and removing the barbell from the rack.

- **Grip.** Two technique guidelines will help you establish a proper grip on the squat. First is the thumb position. Should you have your thumb around the bar or behind the bar? About 60 percent of powerlifters have the thumbs in back, and 40 percent prefer their thumbs around the bar. Obviously, both styles are acceptable, but larger athletes or those with less flexibility should usually lift with their thumbs behind the bar because this grip makes it easier to push the elbows forward and lock in the lower back.

The second grip guideline to consider is the width of the grip. At clinics, we ask attendees to pretend that they have a bar on their shoulders and to get a very narrow grip. Then, we ask them to sit tall, spread their chests, and lock in their lower backs. Next, we tell them to change to a wide grip and lock in their lower backs. When we ask them which grip makes it easier to lock in the lower back, they always respond that it's the wide grip. But athletes need to determine for themselves what works best for them.

Make certain to use as reference points the lines grooved into most Olympic bars about 4 inches (10 centimeters) from the inside collars. For example, you might put your first finger on each line with your thumbs behind the bar. Now you are properly balanced with a wide grip and have some assurance that the bar will remain secure on your shoulders. You are now ready to place the bar on your shoulders. Figure 6.1 illustrates the proper way to grip.

FIGURE 6.1 Perfect grip for the squat.

- **Bar position.** A common mistake is placing the bar too high on the shoulders. Many athletes place the bar right on the neck. That hurts, so they'll use a barbell pad. Most athletes can squat with more weight, greater effectiveness, and more comfort by placing the bar lower on the shoulders. Structural differences in bone length and tendon–muscle attachments may allow some athletes to squat more effectively with high bar placement.

  Some powerlifters place the bar extremely low on the shoulders, perhaps as much as 4 inches (10 centimeters) from the top of the shoulders. This method may give a slight anatomical advantage, or the advantage may result from using a heavy, tight lifting suit or even from a lack of flexibility. Whatever the reason, squatting with extremely low bar placement detracts from overall leg development, which is obviously not helpful to the athlete.

  Most athletes will be able to find a natural groove on the shoulders when they come under the bar in a proper position. We tell them, "Don't put the bar on your neck; put it on your shoulders. Find a groove." In almost every case, if a coach voices these technique cues, athletes will achieve excellent bar placement during their squats.

- **Removing the bar from the rack.** Some high school athletes get psyched up to squat and then position their shoulders 2 to 3 inches (5-8 centimeters) under the bar. Next, with an explosive movement, they jam their shoulders against the bar. Jamming their shoulders against a steel bar from that distance causes bruises on the neck or shoulders. In addition, these athletes often place the bar on their shoulders incorrectly. I've also seen athletes whip a bar off the rack. Many times these athletes are not in solid squatting position as they back up to a ready stance. For those reasons, the few injuries that take place during squatting most often occur while the athlete is taking the bar off the rack or replacing it on the rack, not during the squat exercise itself.

A far superior way to handle the bar is to come under it in a solid power position, making sure that all aspects of technique are correct. To accomplish this, get the bar in the groove on your shoulders. Look straight ahead and spread the chest. The next technique point is critical: Get into your athletic stance directly under the bar. Many athletes stand a foot back and lean forward. Taking that position can cause trouble in the lower back, especially with heavy weight. Now you're ready. Put some pressure on the bar and make sure that everything feels right. If it does, blast off by extending your legs vigorously so the bar lifts off the supports. This explosive movement will not bruise the shoulders because you've already put some pressure on the bar. Because of the explosive movement from the correct position, the bar feels light.

The bar is now off the rack and you are firmly under the weight. At this point, take a short step back with each foot and resume an athletic stance. You are ready to squat. With some squat racks, you may have to take several steps back to clear yourself to squat. Some step-squat racks and peg-squat racks may require many long steps for clearance. Some squat racks have a spotting tier that is too high for parallel squats, thus requiring a long walk back to reach the correct position. Obviously, you are at a disadvantage if you have to do anything more than take a short step back with each foot.

SQUAT TECHNIQUE

The parallel squat can be a tricky lift. Technique and position mean everything. You must execute every technique to perfection when attempting a new max. You must be psyched, but it must be controlled.

The squat has four main phases: the start, the descent, the bottom position, and the upward drive. You must concentrate on perfect technique during all parts of the squat to achieve maximum results.

- **Start.** You should be looking straight ahead at a target. Your mind should be clear and intense, thinking about technique: spreading the chest, locking in the lower back, and performing the descent pattern. Take a huge breath and hold it just before the descent. For a one-rep max, take two breaths—first, a huge breath you hold to let the air settle deep within the rib cavity, and second, a quick breath as you begin the descent to expand the chest even further.

- **Descent.** Descend in an even, controlled pattern. Some athletes descend inch by inch and take forever, which is a mistake. Some athletes rapidly crash down out of control, which is dangerous. By using an even, controlled pattern, your technique will likely be better. Throughout the descent, you should hold your breath. Always spread the chest, lock in the lower back, look at your target, and sit tall.

- **Bottom position.** Squat to the parallel position or slightly below it (figure 6.2a-b). Keep in mind that many athletes squat high, a common flaw that will detract from their performance. By adhering strictly to the parallel position, you will have an advantage in competition. If you squat high, only minimal hamstring and gluteal development will take place, which will limit improvements in speed and jumping. Hitting a correct parallel position is critical for personal and team success, and it is one of the great secrets in this book.

Some football and strength coaches want their athletes to break parallel. The bottom line is that to get proper leg development, athletes must go at least to parallel. Some coaches use the bottom of the thigh,

FIGURE 6.2 You must go to the parallel position or below it to get maximum muscle development. Back squat *(a)* and front squat *(b)*.

not the top of the thigh, as their parallel-squatting reference point. This method creates problems because many athletes with large thighs end up squatting 2 or 3 inches (5-8 centimeters) higher than they would if they used the top of the thigh as the parallel point. These athletes will forgo hamstring and glute development, and standards will become meaningless.

- **Upward drive.** Continue holding your breath when beginning the upward drive from the parallel position. Picture your hips attached to a giant rubber band. As you go down to parallel, you stretch the rubber band to the limit. The instant your hips hit parallel, you release the rubber band. The hips pop upward while you maintain perfect technique.

About halfway up, you pass through the sticking point, the position at which the squat becomes easier. When you reach the sticking point, you should breathe out. Athletes performing a heavy squat will sometimes let out a yell as they expel the air in their lungs. This is perfectly acceptable and probably helps with staying psyched during the lift.

Your eyes should remain fixed on the same point throughout the entire upward drive. When you complete the set, take short, controlled steps back to the rack. Always remain in a solid position as you rack the bar.

SPOTTING

Correct spotting technique is critical to proper execution of the squat. Coaches have the responsibility to teach correct spotting techniques. Three spotters—a back spotter and two side spotters—should be used to ensure success in squatting. The functions of the spotters are threefold. First, the spotters should act as coaches and give correct technique cues. Second, they should act as judges on depth and technique problems. Third, they should be enthusiastic teammates and offer constant encouragement. Spotters should pull the best from their training partners.

Figure 6.3 shows correct spotting positions for the parallel squat. The side spotters are in the correct position for their dual role as coaches and judges. Notice their position. One spotter has his head behind the bar, and the other has his head in front. Spotters must get into these positions to judge the parallel squat. The side spotters should be in squat position on the sides with their hands underneath the bar. If something happens, it usually happens quickly, and the spotters need to be ready. Spotters cannot stand on the sides with their arms crossed. After the lifter completes the set, the side spotters grasp the bar and help the lifter back to the rack.

Spotters need to be vocal in letting their teammates know how they are doing. No lifter can see or hear a nod of the head. Spotters should encourage their teammate during and immediately after the set by offering comments such as "Looking good," "Great job," "Awesome set," "One more rep," or "You can do it." A great set deserves a high five.

The back spotter should place his or her hands firmly on the bar at all times, from the moment the lifter gets under the bar to back out to

FIGURE 6.3 A perfect squat using the six absolutes with spotters in perfect position.

when he or she puts the bar back on the rack after squatting. We are dealing with young athletes, so we want to be as safe as possible. It's unlikely that a spotter will react fast enough to grasp the barbell when there is a problem if he or she does not keep his or her hands on the bar at all times. The back spotter places his or her hands on the bar for two reasons. First, the spotter can easily correct technique, especially when the lifter leans forward. The back spotter just pulls back slightly but firmly to correct the poor position. In addition, the back spotter should talk the lifter through the lift and set. Sometimes powerlifters spot from behind with the arms going under the lifter's armpits to the chest, but this assumes that technique problems are absent.

SOLVING SQUATTING PROBLEMS

Three common mistakes in squatting include knees in, knees forward, and lifting the hips too early. The knees-in problem is more difficult to correct and puts unwanted pressure on the medial collateral ligament. This problem is common among female athletes, whose wider hips cause the upper thigh bones to come inward, as well as among middle school boys who are relatively weak in the lower extremities. When squatting, the knees-in problem will surface on the way up. The knees are usually fine on the way down when squatting. The first step is for the coach to yell "Knees!" to the athlete who is squatting. This is a signal for the athlete to force the knees out.

This signal may not work the first time. If it doesn't, a second correction technique is to tap the outside of the athlete's knee lightly to stimulate the glutes to abduct and externally rotate. This gives the athlete a kinesthetic feel of the problem. The cure usually happens after only a few light taps. If the problem persists, coaches should videotape their athletes performing squats so that they can see themselves. This usually does the trick.

The knees-forward problem often occurs with beginners who lift their heels off the ground during the descent. This error puts harmful stress on the patella and causes the lift to be ineffective. Coaches can correct the knees-forward problem by letting the athlete hold on to a partner's hands for balance, which we call the *squat balance test*. The athlete should sit tall, spread the chest, and keep the elbows and shoulders back. The athlete will then be able to balance with the heels on the ground from a parallel-squat position. The partner should let go after a while to let the athlete have a chance to regain balance from that difficult position.

Surprisingly, most high school athletes can balance themselves after they get the feel of the parallel position with their heels on the ground.

Many bodybuilders squat with the knees forward and the bar positioned high on the neck. They usually lift with a lighter weight and higher reps, along with substituting other exercises for squats such as the leg press, and therefore they may never have a problem. Athletes, however, usually bring the bar back more on the shoulders and want to lift more weight. If the knees continue to come forward with heavier weights, it can be dangerous. The athlete must attempt to sit back more on the hips, with the lower leg being more vertical.

Sometimes, especially with a heavy weight, the hips may come up all right but you lean over. To correct this position, you can try two techniques. First, scoot your hips forward and try to get them underneath the bar. Obviously, you should reexamine the previous technique guidelines for the chest and lower back. The second technique that works extremely well with many athletes is to keep the elbows forward. When you press the elbows forward during a squat, you will tend to have an upright torso with a big chest and a locked-in lower back. The hips will follow the elbows.

BOX SQUAT

BFS has promoted the box squat as a core lift for more than 30 years. It is one of the most effective exercises for developing overall strength and lower-body explosiveness. However, during the first two decades after the BFS program was developed, we had our share of critics who didn't see the value of the exercise and thought it was dangerous. Then the powerlifting community rediscovered the exercise, with champions at all levels and even world-record holders making it a mainstay of their training programs. Its popularity has recently spread among elite strength coaches for all sports. Maybe, just maybe, this an appropriate time to say, "We told you so!"

Before getting into the details of the box squat, we understand that there are coaches who simply refuse to even attempt this exercise. The BFS program is flexible, and there are alternatives. You can use another core lift instead, such as the front squat or even the hip sled. But consider that the box squat is unparalleled for overcoming plateaus, building hip strength and hip tendon strength, improving lower-body explosiveness, and developing the confidence to handle heavier weights and thereby break personal records.

Oh, and there's one more thing. Although the box squat uses more weight than a regular squat, the reduced range of motion of the box squat allows you to recover quickly from the exercise. Just how quickly can you recover? Based on the feedback of the coaches who have won countless championships using the BFS program, you can even box squat heavy the day before an athletic competition without a decrease in performance. Using the Hans Selye model discussed earlier, you will probably even perform better!

Regarding the critics who say the box squat is dangerous, you should have no concerns about safety or liability if you follow our recommendations, which include focusing on perfect technique (rather than on using the heaviest weights possible) and using three attentive spotters. Further, if an athlete is able to use 100 pounds (45 kilograms) more in a box squat compared with a parallel squat, that athlete needs to use a lower box.

I came across the box squat 35 years ago while training in Los Angeles with the world's greatest powerlifters and track athletes (shot-putters, discus throwers, and hammer throwers). Los Angeles at that time was the mecca for amateur power athletes. I'd coach high school track, football, and wrestling and then train in Los Angeles with men such as George Frenn and Jon Cole.

George Frenn taught me how to box squat. George squatted 853 pounds (387 kilograms) in competition and won the national hammer-throw championship three years in a row. That squat was the best achieved by anybody in the world for years, even though George weighed only 242 pounds (110 kilograms). George would box squat once a week and parallel squat once a week. Doing regular squats twice a week was too draining, and George found that he couldn't throw as well in meets or practices. Doing box squats left him with energy for the next day.

Athletes who expect to stay on top of their game need to do sprints and plyometrics and develop the technique of their sport. That routine requires a great deal of time and energy. The box squat allows an athlete to perform a squatting exercise twice a week and still have time and energy to develop athletic abilities. In addition, by adapting to a heavier weight the athlete gains confidence for regular squats.

To perform the box squat, assume an athletic stance and squat carefully under control to a box or a high bench. Take care not to plop down out of control, because doing so could cause injury. Then settle back (rock back) slightly, making certain that your lower back remains concave in a locked-in position. This technique helps shift the stress off the quadriceps so they can contract more forcefully. Then drive forward and up. If you just go down and touch the box or bench, as most athletes do when they perform this exercise, you will develop only the quadriceps, a serious mistake. The final point concerning technique is that you should drive up on your toes in an explosive action as you complete the lift, thereby increasing the range of motion that you are contracting the lower-body muscles. At this final stage, you should have the same feeling you do when blocking, tackling, rebounding, or releasing a track implement (figure 6.4).

FIGURE 6.4 The box squat with correct three-person spotting.

BFS has promoted the box squat as a core lift for more than 30 years. It is one of the most effective exercises for developing overall strength and lower-body explosiveness.

FRONT SQUAT

Many strength coaches believe that the front squat is a better leg exercise than the back squat for athletes. One reason is that because the barbell is positioned on the front of the shoulders rather than on the back, the quads work harder, putting the body in a position commonly used in sports. At the very least, the front squat should be considered a key auxiliary exercise for any athlete. In one survey of top European coaches who were asked to name the three best weight training exercises for sport, the consensus was the power snatch, the incline press, and the front squat.

As for how much emphasis the front squat should receive in an athlete's training, that's up to the strength coach. At BFS, we believe that the back squat should be the primary leg exercise for a young athlete, with the front squat, box squat, and hip sled as key auxiliary exercises. For more experienced athletes with a good base of strength built from years of back squatting, more emphasis could be placed on sport-specific exercises such as front squats and lunges.

One drawback to the front squat is that because holding the weight on the shoulders compresses the chest and makes breathing more labored, it's difficult to perform higher repetitions. Performing more than five repetitions often leads to a breakdown in form and even the possibility of blacking out. But a more important question to ask about this exercise is not whether front squats can replace back squats, but rather why don't more coaches prescribe front squats for their athletes? The answer is pain.

The best way to hold a barbell in a front squat is to use the same grip as you would in a power clean, which is with your hands supinated (palms down) and elbows held high (figure 6.5). Unfortunately, holding the bar in this manner can cause pain in the wrists and elbows if you have relatively long forearms, tightness in the wrists, or—the primary problem—tightness in the upper back or shoulders.

The hardcore Olympic lifters simply say, "Deal with it! Flexibility will come." But others offer special exercises, such as holding the bar while a training partner presses up on the elbows. Some will say, "Just relax your hands and hold on to the bar with your fingertips, making certain you keep the elbows high."

Another technique is to cross your arms in front of you. This method works, but balance can be especially difficult to manage—often you have to focus so much on balancing that it can be hard to put a lot of intensity into the exercise. We've tried several devices that were supposed to make it easier to support the barbell across the shoulders during the front squat, such as the E-Z Squat and the Front Squat Harness. These devices consist of a harness that attaches to the front of the body and allows the weight to be supported on hooks; the athlete holds on to handles for support. The issue with this equipment is that it encourages a rounded back, making it even more difficult to breathe. Also, because the elbows are pointed down with the E-Z Squat, it is possible to jam the elbows into the knees at the bottom position.

The best alternative we've found to the traditional front squat, and one

FIGURE 6.5 The front squat using the power clean grip.

that we unfortunately cannot take credit for, involves the use of lifting straps. Yes, lifting straps.

The front squat described here requires the use of two lifting straps, preferably a pair that has about a foot (30 centimeters) of length after being tied to the bar—some of the quick-release straps Olympic lifters use won't work well for this exercise. Simply hook the straps around the bar at shoulder width or the position that you would normally use for a front squat (see figure 6.6). Generally, this is the same width as the power clean grip.

To perform the exercise, place your shoulders under the bar and grasp the straps with a neutral grip (i.e., palms facing each other). How high up you grab the straps depends upon your flexibility (the less space between the bar and your hands, the better). From this position, simply lift the weight off the squat racks, take a few steps back, and bend the knees until the thighs are at least parallel to the floor, similar to the back squat. Now reverse directions to return to the start. You'll find that you can keep your elbows high and the weight securely on your shoulders with this method. The only drawback is it can be difficult to replace the bar on the racks, so you should have a spotter assist you.

There is less stress on the wrists for two reasons: The upper arms do not have to be bent back as far as with a regular front squat, and the wrists are in a neutral position as opposed to the supinated position (palms up) used with regular front squatting.

Another advantage of this exercise is that if you are not capable of performing front squats, it will improve your flexibility until such time as you are able to perform front squats. Start by holding the top end of the straps, and as your flexibility improves, move your hands close to the bottom. Eventually you should be able to smoothly transition into regular front squats, if this is your desire.

How much can athletes lift in the front squat? We've heard reports of numerous top weightlifters such as Paul Anderson, Vladimir Marchuk, and Mark Henry going all the way down and using no special equipment while lifting over 700 pounds (318 kilograms). Three-time Olympic champion Pyrros Dimas of Greece and

FIGURE 6.6 The use of lifting straps can help if you experience pain in the wrists or elbows when performing the front squat.

Dursun Sevinc of Turkey, both weighing 187 pounds (85 kilograms), have reportedly lifted more than 600 pounds (272 kilograms) in this exercise. Generally, however, the ratio of back squat to front squat should be about 70 to 80 percent if you are going to equal depth in both exercises.

The front squat is a superior exercise, and many coaches even prefer it to the back squat. At BFS, we've promoted it as a key auxiliary lower-body exercise because it has advantages in leg development and, in some cases, sport specificity. Whether you make front squats a major part of your training or just throw them into your workout occasionally for variety, using lifting straps will help make performing the squats a lot easier—and pain free as well.

VARIATIONS

Other acceptable squat variations are the high-bar bodybuilding, or Olympic-style, squat; the safe-bar squat; and the hip sled. In the high-bar bodybuilding squat, athletes use less weight than they do in the parallel squat, and some athletes who choose this option go several inches below parallel. We do not emphasize this variation, but we recognize its acceptability for those who perform it with good technique.

The hip sled works the major lower-body muscles in a multijoint fashion without tiring the lower back. The hip sled is mounted on incline rails and has padded steel appendages for the shoulders and a footplate at the bottom (figure 6.7). The athlete enters the machine facedown and places the shoulders between the appendages and the feet shoulder width apart

FIGURE 6.7 Hip sled.

on the footplate. Keeping the back arched, the athlete straightens the legs to perform the movement (figure 6.8). Because relatively little stability is required to perform this exercise and because the sled is placed at an incline, athletes can often use more weight on this exercise than they do on the box squat. Care must be taken not to bounce the weight out of the bottom position to use more weight, because doing so can stress the lower back and knees.

FIGURE 6.8 Squat thrust using a hip sled.

LIFTING CHAINS

The rationale for using lifting chains is covered in detail in the chapter on the bench press. The biggest difference is that because the chain is lifted higher off the ground than during the bench press, the amount of resistance applied to the barbell during the lift is greater (figure 6.9).

FIGURE 6.9 Lifting chains can be used in all variations of the squat.

Those are the basics of productive squatting. If you follow the guidelines closely, you'll develop unbelievably strong quads, glutes, and hamstrings, a combination that translates into reduced susceptibility to injury, improved power, and greater athletic performance.

CHAPTER 7

Power Clean and Quick Lifts

The power clean is vital to athletes. To develop ability to the highest levels, athletes must perform one or more quick lifts such as power cleans and power snatches. Quick lifts can be performed with a squat style (dropping into a full squat when the weight is racked to the shoulders) or a power style (in which there is only a slight bend in the knees).

The power clean is the most popular quick lift, and because we base our Bigger Faster Stronger (BFS) standards on it, we recommend it be performed first in our workouts. The power clean develops jumping ability, explosiveness, aggressiveness, and overall athleticism by teaching athletes how to effectively use their major muscle groups in a coordinated fashion. Every muscle comes into play, and when done correctly, every muscle fires in proper sequence. This summation of forces creates maximum power. However, this invaluable exercise has had its critics.

INJURY AND JOINT CONCERNS

For many years the power clean has been attacked by those who thought it had little value for athletes, those who thought it was dangerous, and those who thought it was too difficult to teach. The attackers of the power clean were wrong, and the survival of the exercise has benefited those who want to run faster, jump higher, and be more powerful overall. So, why the resistance? Perhaps, as with many other aspects of life, you have to follow the money.

Much of the criticism about the power clean came from companies that sold exercise machines, such as that of the late Arthur Jones, inventor of the popular Nautilus machines. Although machines have their place in strength and conditioning programs, especially in the area of injury rehabilitation, many manufacturers aggressively campaigned against the power clean in order to sell more machines. After all, if you're outfitting a gym with platforms and free weights, manufacturers won't be able to sell you as many machines!

A recent survey involving 137 Division I coaches found that 85 percent used Olympic lifting movements such as the power clean to train their athletes. In the National Football League (NFL), that percentage was 88 percent. High school football programs are also catching on, especially those that enjoy a tradition of victory.

When BFS editor-in-chief Kim Goss was a strength coach for the Air Force Academy (1987-1994), he enlisted the help of the university's math department to conduct an experiment to determine which strength training exercises had the highest correlation to the ability to play football. For three years, he compiled the results of the top three athletes on the depth chart for each position and their maxes on our core and auxiliary exercises. For defensive and offensive linemen, as well as for almost all positions, the exercise that had the highest correlation to playing ability was the power clean.

The reason for these results is simple. Linemen need to be able to express a high level of strength quickly. During the middle of a power clean, the legs straighten and then rebend before straightening again. This prestretching of the muscles creates a plyometric effect that enables the body to use stored energy to move faster. As such, the power clean is one of the best exercises for improving what sport scientists refer to as the rate of force development. This is in contrast to conventional power lifts such as squats, which for safety reasons require more time to decelerate the weight; the only time maximum force can be exerted is at the beginning of those exercises. And practical evidence published in peer-reviewed journals supports the idea that power cleans are a superior exercise for developing power.

For example, in 2004, researchers at the Department of Health and Exercise Science at the College of New Jersey conducted a 15-week study on weightlifting exercises involving 20 Division III college players. One group focused on powerlifting exercises such as the squat, while the other group focused on Olympic lifting exercises such as the power clean. Although both groups showed improvements in the vertical jump, a standard test for athletic power, the authors said, "Results suggest that [Olympic lifting] can provide a significant advantage over [powerlifting] in vertical jump performance changes."

For those athletes seeking to improve muscle mass, the power clean is also an effective exercise. There are two types of fast-twitch muscles fibers that can increase in size: type IIa and the more powerful type IIb. Type IIb fibers respond better to explosive lifts such as the power clean, and much of the massive development of the trapezoids, lower back, and hamstrings on Olympic lifters is due to the development of type IIb fibers. So if you want as much functional muscle mass as possible for sport, you need to perform the power clean.

But what about the idea that the power clean is dangerous? Again going back to Coach Goss' days at the Air Force Academy, data collected from our athletic trainers showed that the total number of injuries for the first 5 years I coached there had decreased by 60 percent! He was solely responsible for designing the workouts for the football team, and a feature of his workout programs was extensive use of the power clean. If this lift was so dangerous, how can one account for such results? I have a theory about this—and a story.

During a power clean, the athlete not only must explosively lift the weight but also must catch it. In effect, power cleans teach athletes to rapidly control the impact, or disrupted force, that occurs during the lift. When you consider the ever-increasing numbers of athletes suffering ACL injuries, you can see how valuable it is to be able to handle the dynamic, disrupted forces that occur at the ankle and knee during athletic competition. Further, the faster athletes can handle these disrupted forces, the quicker they will be able to move on the court or in the field.

Finally, the power clean and other quick lifts are economical exercises, meaning they work many muscle groups simultaneously. To achieve a similar training effect with conventional exercises, athletes would have to perform a leg press, back extension, calf raise, upright row, and a biceps curl—and even then they would be neglecting a few muscles. Time is a major limiting factor in many athletic programs, so it's important to use exercises such as the power clean that give you the most bang for your buck. Further, the power clean works the legs and hips with a rotary action (as the hips move forward and down during the middle of the pull) that is specific to the movements that occur in sport.

I saw a dramatic example of the benefits of the power clean when I worked with Mark Eaton of the Utah Jazz. When he was cleaning only 115 pounds (52 kilograms), he would wimp it up, and that's how he looked when rebounding and when blocking shots. But as his technique improved, he developed a much more aggressive attitude toward the clean. Later, he cleaned 250 pounds (113 kilograms) and would let out a roar and explode through the lift. Mark led the NBA in blocked shots and was an NBA all-star in 1989. He made so much progress that I wanted to put a football helmet on him!

Is the power clean difficult to teach? Certainly not, if you have the proper educational materials and coaches who know how to teach it. BFS currently gives more than 400 clinics a year to young athletes and has been doing so for over 30 years. The power clean is taught in all these clinics, and we often see athletes who have never performed this exercise come away with sound technique that will quickly lead to gains in athletic performance. Further, at our certification clinics, we ensure quality instruction, because coaches must demonstrate not only that they can perform the power clean but also that they can teach it.

Despite its critics, the power clean has proven to be an exercise that can be safe, easy to teach, and one of the most important exercises for achieving physical superiority. It will improve jumping ability, explosiveness, and overall coordination.

SAFETY GUIDELINES

Before explaining how to perform the power clean, you need to be aware of some general safety guidelines.

First, never perform more than five reps during a set. The power clean is a complex lift, and it is difficult to perform higher reps and maintain good technique. Also, using higher reps will not allow you to train the most fast-twitch muscle fibers.

Second, because it is easy to overtrain these muscle fibers with the power clean, you may not be able to use maximal weights more than once a week with the exercise. During the lighter workouts, focus on mastering technique and increasing lifting speed.

Third, do not bounce the bar on the floor between reps, even when using rubber bumper plates. Although this technique may enable you to lift more weight, it is stressful on the spine. Further, it does not develop the glutes and hamstrings as effectively as starting the lift from a complete stop.

We recommend learning the power clean from an experienced strength coach who has performed quick lifts and from studying our technique videos. Having said that, here are five technique points that will help ensure that you are performing the lift correctly.

PRELIFT TECHNIQUE

- **Start with a jump stance.** The power clean is basically a jump with weights, and as such you should start the lift from a jump stance (figure 7.1). Grasp the bar with your arms straight, hands about shoulder width apart, with your elbows in line with your knees. It's important to keep the bar close to your shins not just to enable you to lift more weight but also to protect your lower back. At clinics, a general guideline we tell athletes is to "feel the steel."

- **Lock in your lower back.** Starting with the back in a concave position will allow you to transfer power from your lower body to the barbell. Spread your chest! Another technique tip to help achieve this position is to keep the chin up (i.e., eyes on target).

FIGURE 7.1 The power clean starting position is a jump stance with the back in a concave position and the chest spread.

LIFT TECHNIQUE

- **Start the pull with your legs and hips.** The arms and shoulders are used at the top of the pull, not the start. You want to keep your arms straight at the start of the pull and not jerk the weight off the floor, instead moving the barbell upward with the strength of your legs and hips (figure 7.2a).

- **Keep the bar close to your body as you start the pull.** To perform the exercise with maximum explosiveness and safety, you must keep the barbell close to the body at all times. To do this, at the start of the pull the barbell will actually be moving slightly backward, not straight up and down. When the barbell reaches the middle of the thighs, your shoulders should be slightly in front of the barbell and you will be in a great position to explode upward as you would in a vertical jump (figure 7.2b).

- **Finish the pull with your elbows high.** When the bar passes the knees, the shoulders and arms will start to apply force to the barbell. To keep the bar moving straight up, keep your shoulders close to your ears and your elbows high (figure 7.2c). These tips will also help keep the barbell close to your body as you begin the catch portion of the exercise.

- **Snap explosively into the catch position.** When the barbell reaches maximum height, your elbows should snap forward under the bar and your feet should pop out into an athletic stance (figure 7.2d). In the catch position, your back should still be in a concave position.

FIGURE 7.2 Start the pull with your legs and hips *(a)*. Keep the bar close to your body as you start the pull and use the arms and shoulders at the top of the pull, during the shrug, not the start *(b)*. Finish the pull with your elbows high *(c)* then snap explosively into catch position *(d)*.

SPOTTING

Experienced athletes are not spotted on quick lifts because it can be dangerous for the spotter to try to catch a snatch or a power clean and because the movements are so quick that any interference by the spotter could result in a shift in the athlete's position that could cause injury. Spotters are not required, but rubber-coated or solid rubber bumper barbell plates are necessary so that the athlete can drop the weight without ruining the barbell or the platform.

With beginners who are using light weights and just learning the lifts, it is permissible to have a spotter standing behind the athlete. Beginners have a tendency to fall backward, and if there is not enough clearance behind them (often platforms are set up close to walls), they could be seriously injured. A spotter would simply place the hands in front as if performing a standing push-up and stand behind the athlete to prevent the athlete from falling backward by pushing lightly against the upper back. Again, spotting should only be performed on the power clean with beginners who are using light weights.

VARIATION: THE POWER SNATCH

The power snatch is an advanced auxiliary exercise that can be used in place of the power clean; it uses essentially the same muscles and also develops explosiveness. The main difference between the two lifts is that instead of bringing the barbell to rest on the shoulders, you flip the weight overhead. Also, the power snatch uses a wider grip.

We recommend performing the power clean first because you can use heavier weight and develop more muscle mass and it is easier for most athletes to learn. But once you've mastered the power clean, the power snatch is relatively easy to master because the movement is similar.

There are several reasons to try the power snatch. First, it tends to be easier on the wrists and elbows than the power clean and requires less flexibility in the upper back. Some athletes, especially those with relatively long lower arms compared to their upper arms, find that racking the bar is extremely uncomfortable. There's no such problem with the power snatch.

The power snatch more aggressively works the muscles that externally rotate the shoulders. In sports such as baseball and swimming, the muscles that internally rotate the shoulders often become overdeveloped in relation to those that externally rotate the shoulders. This imbalance contributes to an unnatural, forward head posture that makes the shoulders more susceptible to injury. Rather than performing several boring isolation exercises for the rotator cuff to deal with this problem, athletes can simply add the power snatch to their workouts.

Because a lighter weight is used, the power snatch is a much faster lift than the power clean. This makes it ideal for improving jumping ability. Also, because a wider grip is used, it develops the hamstrings, glutes, and lower back muscles through a greater range of motion.

With the power snatch, you assume the same position as the power clean, but with your arms wider apart. As a general guideline, your arms should be at a 45-degree angle from the midline of the body when the barbell is overhead; this is the snatch grip. With the hands wider, you will need to bend your legs more at the start. Following are instructions for how to perform the lift. Note that these instructions share many of the same technical aspects as the power clean.

PRELIFT TECHNIQUE

- **Start with a jump stance.** As with the power clean, the power snatch is basically a jump with weights, and as such you should start the lift from a jump stance. Grasp the bar with a snatch grip, with your arms straight and your elbows in line with your knees. Keep the bar close to your shins so that you can lift more weight and protect your lower back. In other words, feel the steel.
- **Lock in your lower back and spread your chest.** Starting with your back in a concave position allows you to transfer power from the lower body to the barbell. Keep the chin up (i.e., eyes on target).

LIFT TECHNIQUE

- **Start the pull with your legs and hips.** The arms and shoulders are used at the top of the pull, not the start. You want to keep your arms straight at the start of the pull and not jerk the weight off the floor, instead moving the barbell up with the strength of your legs and hips.
- **Keep the bar close to your body as you start the pull.** To perform the exercise with maximum explosiveness and safety, you must keep the barbell close to the body at all times. To do this, at the start of the pull the barbell will actually be moving slightly backward, not straight up and down. When the barbell reaches the middle of the thighs, the shoulders will be slightly in front of the barbell and you will be in a great position to explode upward as you would in a vertical jump.

- **Finish the pull with your elbows high.** When the bar passes the knees, the shoulders and arms will start to apply force to the barbell. To keep the bar moving straight up, keep your shoulders close to your ears and your elbows high. These tips will also help keep the barbell close to your body as you begin the catch.
- **Snap explosively into the catch position.** When the barbell reaches maximum height, your shoulders should rotate backward so that your arms can continue moving above and slightly behind your head as your feet pop out into an athletic stance (figure 7.3). In the catch position, your back should still be in a concave position.

The power snatch is a fun lift for athletes to perform because the barbell travels extremely fast through a great range of motion. Give it a try sometime and we're sure you'll agree that the power snatch is a great lift to add to your program.

FIGURE 7.3 The power snatch technique is nearly identical to the power clean until the catch stage, when your shoulders should rotate backward so that your arms can continue moving above and slightly behind your head as your feet pop out into an athletic stance.

Power Clean High

One of the interesting aspects of the BFS program is that our success stories often repeat themselves. Take, for example, the story of David Harvey-Bowen.

David is a graduate of Churchville-Chili Senior High School, located just outside Rochester, New York. We did our first article about David when he was in ninth grade and he power cleaned 340 pounds (154 kilograms), bench-pressed 355 pounds (161 kilograms), and squatted 605 pounds (274 kilograms). In high school at a body weight of 242 pounds (110 kilograms), he set several United States Powerlifting Federation (USPF) records with a 430-pound (195-kilogram) bench,

One of the most famous graduates of Churchville-Chili High School is David Harvey-Bowen, our 1998 BFS Male High School Athlete of the Year. David could power clean 340 pounds in ninth grade, and by late high school he did 412.

720-pound (327-kilogram) squat, and 690-pound (313-kilogram) deadlift; he could also power clean 412 pounds (187 kilograms). On the gridiron, David was an impressive running back, rushing for 1,420 yards (1,298 meters) and 22 touchdowns in his senior season. Whew!

In 1998, BFS honored David's accomplishments in athletics and in the weight room by naming him the BFS Male Athlete of the Year. David went on to accept a scholarship to Western Kentucky University, and his high school coach, Paul Dick, knew that it would be some time before he saw talent of the caliber of David Harvey-Bowen again. That's why we were excited when Coach Dick called us and said that he had another story for us.

The difference this time is that Coach Dick doesn't have just one strong football player who can power clean major household appliances; he has six of them! Specifically, Churchville-Chili High School went into the 2007 season with a half-dozen athletes who could power clean at least 300 pounds (136 kilograms), with a best of 350 pounds (159 kilograms)!

"Our players knew about David—we still have pictures and articles about him displayed in our weight room—and his success gave our team an understanding of what can be accomplished by hard work and following a sound weight training program," says Dick. That understanding was a major reason why Dick's teams have made the semifinals or higher for the football state championships for five years in a row, finishing 8-1 in 2006. Further, in the last 11 years, eight of Dick's athletes at Churchville-Chili High have earned Division I scholarships—a remarkable achievement for any high school at any level. But it wasn't always this way.

Churchville-Chili High School went into the 2007 season with a half-dozen athletes who could power clean at least 300 pounds.

Starting From Square One

Coach Dick was a student teacher at Churchville-Chili in 1987 but he wasn't involved in football, and with good reason. The school didn't have a football team, and it never had.

"When I started my student teaching, we were the largest school in New York that didn't have a football team," says Dick. "I remember asking the athletic director at the time if we would ever have football at this school, and his answer—which I remember clearly to this day because it was so emphatically negative—was that we will never have a football program and we shouldn't because we don't get the kind of kids who can support a football team. Two years later the school hired a new athletic director who had the opposite attitude, and he passed a budget that would allow us to field a team."

Dick recalls that the major problem that first year was not getting kids to come out for football but that the kids didn't know what was expected of them to play the game. He explains, "We had a lot of kids, but most had no understanding about the game. For example, they didn't know all the things they had to do to play, such as working hard in the weight room in the off-season." As a result, that first season ended with a 0-9 record, followed by a 1-8 season and a 2-7 season. But Dick's enthusiasm and patience paid off, and by David Harvey-Bowen's senior year the team finished 7-3 and started gaining respect in their conference.

> continued

> continued

Power Clean Factor

Coach Dick is a big fan of explosive movements for football, such as the power clean and power snatch. And no athlete could ask for a better teacher or role model.

In 1988, Coach Dick competed in the Olympic trials as a heavyweight (242 pounds [110 kilograms] body weight). He took a silver medal in the snatch, lifting 314 pounds (142 kilograms), and he clean and jerked 402 pounds (182 kilograms) to earn the bronze overall. What's more, he got his start with BFS. "In my first year of college football I remember watching the Bigger Faster Stronger video, and that's how I got introduced to power cleans—I had never done the lift before," he says.

Because of the success that he and his college football team had using BFS principles, Dick has always been a fan of BFS and of explosive lifting. In addition to encouraging his athletes to lift big weights in the power clean, he promotes the power snatch: "It helps shoulder stability, and the kids enjoy it, but I also found that the power snatch helps teach the kids to keep the barbell close to the body. If athletes tend to let the bar drift out in the power clean, they resolve the problem after focusing on the power snatch for a time."

In recent years, one change that Dick made to his program was to implement the BFS readiness program with the seventh and eighth graders who will eventually attend the high school. "Just before we started becoming successful, we'd had some issues getting our younger kids into the weight room, so we really bought into the readiness program. And I want to say this: One of the best things we ever did was buy the 15-pound [7-kilogram] Aluma-Lite barbells."

"What we realized is that when you have young kids in the weight room and put a 45-pound [20-kilogram] bar in their hands for them to start working out, some kids struggle to hit the right position at the start from the hang position, and this is discouraging to them. The 15-pound [7-kilogram] bar allows them to get into the correct position and learn proper technique; and then when we add the 10-pound [4.5-kilogram] bumpers, the weight is still only 35 pounds [16 kilograms]."

In 2007, Dick returned 18 of 22 starters and expected at least four of his current seniors to earn college scholarships, so his expectations for the squad were high. What's more, those six athletes who can clean over 300 pounds (136 kilograms) are all juniors, so he doesn't expect to have to do much rebuilding in 2008. "Certainly these kids have talent to play the game, but there's no doubt about it," he says. "Our weight program has played a big role in the success of our athletic program."

CHAPTER 8

Hex-Bar Deadlift and Deadlift Variations

The hex-bar deadlift strengthens the lower back, hamstrings, thighs, torso, and trapezoids. Because it strengthens so many large muscle groups, it is a key exercise in the BFS program.

In the early years of BFS, athletes performed both the deadlift and the power clean on the same day. As the BFS program evolved, we decided to replace the deadlift with the hex-bar deadlift, an exercise performed with a hexagonal barbell that weighs 45 pounds (20 kilograms). The hexagonal shape allows the lifter to perform exercises from inside the bar. Handgrips strategically placed on the ends of the bar enable the weight on the bar to be in perfect alignment with the power line at all times. There are four basic types of hex bars: the hex bar, the combo hex bar, the mega hex bar, and the youth hex bar. The combo and mega hex bars can be flipped over to accommodate taller athletes. The mega hex bar weighs 75 pounds and is designed for exceptional strong individuals and can hold over 800 pounds in plates. The youth hex bar only weighs 15 pounds and is designed for young athletes. Figure 8.1a through d shows the different types of hex bars.

The power line is an imaginary line that runs up through the lifter's center mass. Executing the deadlift movement through the power line enables athletes to develop maximum power and reduces risk of injury. The farther the weight diverges from the power line, the more power the lifter loses. For example, how long can you hold a 45-pound (20-kilogram) bar with your arms straight down and the bar resting against your

FIGURE 8.1 There are four basic types of hex bars: the hex bar (a), the combo hex bar (b), the mega hex bar (c), and the youth hex bar (d).

thighs? Probably for a long time. Now try holding the bar about a foot (30 centimeters) out from your thighs. Doing that is much harder. The farther the bar gets from center mass, the harder it is to hold and the more power is lost. In addition, because the hex bar makes using correct technique easy, a spotter is not necessary.

INJURY AND JOINT CONCERNS

Although the deadlift can still be used in the BFS program as an auxiliary lift, we've found the hex-bar deadlift to be a superior exercise. Because the torso is more upright than it is with the regular deadlift, compression forces on the spine and stress on the lower back are reduced. This difference makes it possible for athletes to work the lower back hard every week, whereas such frequency of training with the regular deadlift often results in overtraining. The hex bar also lends itself to performing shrugs because the bar does not contact the thighs.

In addition, we don't recommend the regular deadlift for young athletes because they tend to round their lower back. This means the back muscles are relaxed and the weight is hanging by the ligaments.

Conquering fear of the deadlift is the purpose of using the hex bar. The deadlift is a superb exercise for the lower body and torso, but for years fear has overshadowed its great benefits. Coaches and athletes have been afraid of the heavy weight and difficult technique associated with the deadlift. The key to conquering this fear is proper technique. As with all lifts, proper technique will eliminate potential injury. With the hex bar, executing great technique has never been easier. The hex bar makes doing the deadlift easy and fun for anyone.

The hex bar is a space saver. It is only 56 inches (142 centimeters) long, compared with the 86 inches (218 centimeters) of space that regular Olympic bars occupy. This compactness allows placement of many hex bar stations in a small area. In addition, the shorter length of the bar decreases the distance of the weight from the lifter, giving the lifter more control and balance for a more efficient, intense workout.

Prior to the development of the hex bar, athletes used a trap bar. The hex bar proved to be a better design because it gave the athlete more room for the feet and was more stable.

Hex-bar workouts are also fast. On one of my first workouts with the hex bar, I did five sets of five reps, going up to 375 pounds (170 kilograms). The workout took much less time than a squat or deadlift workout would—only eight minutes. I was so sore the next day in my glutes, hamstrings, and traps that I could hardly walk. The workout was just like a heavy parallel squat workout when I hadn't squatted for a while, but my lower back felt great. I was impressed.

PRELIFT TECHNIQUE

- **Start with a jump stance.** To perform the deadlift with the hex or high hex bar, step into the center of the hexagon and assume the jump stance. Then squat and grab the handgrips on both sides of the bar, making sure to place the hands squarely in the middle of the handles for balance.
- **Lock in your lower back.** Lower the hips, spread the chest, lock the lower back in place, keep the head up with the eyes forward, and put the knees directly over the feet.

LIFT TECHNIQUE

- **Lift the bar straight up through the power line using the legs.** Because of the unique design of the hex bar, you can keep the weight along the power line throughout the entire lift (figure 8.2*a-c*). Once you have stood up completely, the first repetition is complete and you are ready for the next rep.

- **As in all lifts, the head should be up and the chin stretched away from the chest.** If the chin touches the chest, the entire body will become dangerously out of position. This technique reduces the amount of weight that the athlete can lift and, more important, is dangerous and can cause injury to the lower back.

FIGURE 8.2 When performing the hex-bar deadlift, start in a jump stance, with your lower back locked *(a)*, then lift the bar straight up through the power line using the legs *(b-c)*.

- **Squat, keeping the lower back locked in, the chest spread, and the eyes on target.** To minimize back strain, bounce the weights slightly off the floor when doing repetitions. Pausing in the down position after each rep is not necessary or desirable.

A variation of the hex bar is the high hex bar. They are identical except that the high hex bar has elevated handgrips. The higher starting position allowed by the high hex bar makes executing exercises easier for beginning lifters and tall lifters. The higher starting position also enables you to use heavier weights in the exercise.

VARIATIONS

The straight-leg and spotted deadlifts are both great variations of the hex-bar deadlift to incorporate into a program to add variety.

Straight-Leg Deadlift

The BFS straight-leg deadlift is a high priority auxiliary lift. We think of this lift as a stretching exercise. Therefore, our recommended technique is to use a light weight and perform every rep slowly, controlled, and deep. Middle school boys and girls should use 45 pounds (20 kilograms) or less. Most high school female athletes should use between 45 and 65 pounds (20-30 kilograms). Strong, mature female high school athletes could use up to a maximum of 95 pounds (43 kilograms). Strong, mature male high school athletes could use up to a maximum of 135 pounds (61 kilograms). The absolute max athletes should use is 40 percent of their parallel squat. Do two sets of 10 repetitions two times per week, and do not try to do a little more each week. Keep the poundage the same.

Begin the straight-leg deadlift in a slow and controlled movement. Keep the legs straight with the knees locked (not hyperextended) at all times (see figure 8.3). When you do a hamstring stretch, you can't bend the knees at all; it is the same in the BFS straight-leg deadlift. You can pause at the bottom before coming back up. To get a deeper stretch, perform the lift while standing on a low platform.

FIGURE 8.3 The straight-leg deadlift on a low platform.

Spotted Deadlift

Once or twice a year it's a great idea to put on an event for your team featuring the deadlift with a spotter. The coach and all team members should have a wild max-out party. As each team member takes a turn, everyone shouts, "Go, go, go!" This kind of event can generate awesome intensity. We do this at BFS clinics, and the average high school football player can lift 400 pounds (181 kilograms). Our all-state standard is 500 pounds (227 kilograms), and the all-American standard is 600 pounds (272 kilograms).

In powerlifting contests, of course, athletes cannot use a spotter for the deadlift. Schools that keep records of weights for the deadlift should establish records from reps in which a spotter is not used. A spotter usually assists by lifting 50 to 75 pounds (23-34 kilograms), a contribution that would invalidate an athlete's record. During regular training, using a spotter is vital for safety. With sufficient training, athletes will be ready to lift unassisted when it's time for contests and setting records.

With the spotted deadlift, the spotter presses down with one hand on the lower back and hooks the other around the lifter's shoulder and chest. The spotter secures the crook of the elbow against the shoulder and places the fist or hand firmly against the middle of the chest. This technique enables the spotter to apply pressure to the lower back to prevent it from rounding. The spotting technique is merely to ensure that the lower back does not round. The spotter and lifter should coordinate the lift, perhaps by the spotter saying, "One, two, up."

FIGURE 8.4 The proper spotting position for the spotted deadlift.

As the lift begins, the spotter pulls up and back while pushing on the lower back (see figure 8.4). This technique is important for safety. The spotter pulls back to get the weight shifted toward the lifter's heels. When high school athletes deadlift by themselves, the weight often shifts toward the toes. This shift not only reduces the amount of weight lifted but also can injure the lower back. When the weight shifts back toward the heels, athletes can normally deadlift in complete safety.

As with all BFS core lifts, keeping records and setting goals is important. For male athletes, the BFS varsity standard for the hex-bar deadlift or spotted deadlift is 400 pounds (181 kilograms), the all-state standard is 500 pounds (227 kilograms), and the all-American standard is 600 pounds (272 kilograms). Female athletes have a varsity standard of 235 pounds (107 kilograms), an all-state standard of 325 pounds (147 kilograms), and an all-American standard of 415 pounds (188 kilograms).

Now let's go get some records!

The Lady Flames Heat Up the Court

Ask any number of high school coaches when was the last time they worked only 40 hours in a week, and they'll usually respond with laughter. Ever-increasing responsibilities and relatively low pay at this level are challenges, and high school coaches are burning out a lot quicker than they did in the past. For girls basketball coach Erin Aitken, however, that's not a problem she's likely to face anytime soon. Winning championships and postseason honors is providing all the motivation she needs.

The hex-bar deadlift is a key exercise in the Lady Flames strength and conditioning program.

Aitken is having the time of her life as the head coach of girls basketball at Lodi High School in Lodi, California. This school must make quite an impression on its students, because approximately half the teachers at Lodi, including Aitken, are Lodi graduates. The girls junior varsity coach at Lodi, Cal Krienke, was even Aitken's high school coach! With such a history of loyalty and enthusiasm, it's only natural that last season the Lady Flames had an undefeated season in league play, with a 23-5 overall record.

To gain insight into the success at Lodi High School, we contacted Coach Aitken, who took time out to answer our questions.

BFS: Was it awkward at first coming back to the school that you graduated from?

> continued

> *continued*

Aitken: No, actually I was very excited. To me this was a dream come true, and besides, it's great to relive your playing days and the coaches you played for.

BFS: How did you get involved with BFS?

Aitken: BFS clinician Mark Beckham did a clinic for us, and it really helped the football team. Now other sports are using BFS, and it's really taken off.

BFS: Was there resistance at first from your girls about weight training?

Aitken: The first thing I emphasized was technique; but when the girls started going up in weight, many of them were apprehensive. I remember that as the girls started working hard and getting stronger, there were ridiculous rumors going around in school that they were doing steroids, so I decided to have the girls work out at the same time as the football team. Since then, the attitude toward the girls lifting on campus has been positive.

BFS: Do you believe that you have an advantage over a male coach in coaching girls?

Aitken: Yes, in the sense that I believe it's important for girls to have good female role models. And because I can demonstrate the lifts and I'm not bulky, that helps deal with the myth about lifting making girls big and muscular.

BFS: Do you think it's a mistake to have a girl who shows talent in one sport participate in specialized sport camps and additional leagues in that sport?

Aitken: Obviously, I want my teams to win, but I also want these kids to enjoy other sports. Other than weight training, I do very limited sport-specific activities with my athletes. I do have players who go and play in AAU, but I think this leads to overtraining and burnout.

BFS: How important is it to participate in these camps and leagues to get more exposure to college scouts?

Aitken: I believe if you have talent, people are going to know about you and you don't have to spend thousands of dollars to be on competitive teams. If there is a specific college that one of my kids wants to try to get into, I tell her to go ahead and go to that school's camp—I'll even contact the coach to help set it up. I've also found that college coaches want to recruit all-around good athletes, not just basketball players—they want to see how you move on a soccer field, say, or a volleyball court.

BFS: Have you had to deal much with injuries with your athletes?

Aitken: We had one sprained ankle this year, and she was a transfer student who had had no weight training experience. The last major injury we had was three years ago: A girl tore her ACL, but this girl had just started weight training with us. Other than that, girls basketball has had no other injuries. I believe this is due in part to preventative measures, such as doing the BFS program and using ankle braces.

BFS: Ankle injuries are common in girls basketball. Is there any specific exercise you believe is especially important for the sport?

Aitken: I really love the dot drill for females because it's a single-leg exercise and develops ankle strength and balance. I also believe that plyometrics helps strengthen the ankles, and obviously the weight training is important. For auxiliaries for basketball, I like snatches and push presses.

BFS: Do you believe that females have such a high rate of knee injuries, especially ACL tears, due to their anatomy or due to a lack of proper conditioning?

Aitken: I believe it's a combination of both, but more so a lack of strength training in getting the ideal quad-to-hamstring ratio. Also, girls are much more competitive now, and often this leads to overtraining, which can cause injury.

BFS: Besides fewer injuries, have you noticed anything different in the way the girls play that might be attributed to your strength and conditioning program?

Aitken: One thing I've really noticed since we started the BFS program is that we don't have nearly the amount of tied-up balls that cause jump balls. It's unbelievable the number of tied-up balls you have at the high school level, but our girls are getting the loose balls because they are strong enough to literally rip the ball out of opponents' arms. And the weight training has been tremendous for the confidence level of the girls—they are more willing to take risks. I constantly tell my players, "If you can squat 200 pounds [91 kilograms], are you trying to tell me that those girls can knock you out of the way?" And they look at me and say, "Yeah, Coach, you're right!"

CHAPTER 9

Bench Press and Bench Press Variations

Just as the squat is the king of lower-body exercises, the bench press is at the top for its ability to develop overall strength in the upper body—the chest, shoulders, and triceps. Although some strength coaches choose to leave it out of their programs, we believe that the bench press is essential.

For one thing, the standards are easily recognizable. Athletes want to work harder to achieve the magic standards of benching 200, 300, 400, or 500 pounds (91, 136, 181, or 227 kilograms). Although the value of a 600-pound (272-kilogram) bench press is questionable, the great male champions of size, strength, and speed seem to have the ability to bench-press at least 400 pounds (181 kilograms). This exercise is especially important for female athletes because they carry proportionately less muscle mass in the upper body than males do. This gap in strength often compromises their ability to play sports at a high level. The standards we use for women are 100, 150, 200, and 250 pounds (45, 68, 92, and 113 kilograms). Thus, a high school coach should be pleased to see a girl bench-press 100 pounds (45 kilograms). A bench of 150 pounds (68 kilograms) is a rare accomplishment for a high school girl, and 200 pounds (91 kilograms) is a weight few women other than college throwers can lift.

BENCH PRESS AND INJURIES

Most injuries in bench-pressing come from improper spotting. When a lifter misses a repetition, the barbell will become pinned on the chest and the lifter can only remove the barbell by rolling it down the legs or tilting the weight to the side to allow the plates to fall off. This is why we do not recommend bench-pressing alone, even if the weight is light. However, a single spotter may not be enough with heavy weights—there are several powerlifters now who have bench-pressed over 1,000 pounds (454 kilograms) in competition!

Much of the risk of the bench press can be reduced by bench-pressing inside a power rack, as long as the safety supports are adjusted properly so that athletes can squeeze themselves out from underneath the supports. Also, having additional bar supports set lower will help because often athletes can press the weight partially off their chest. However, removing a barbell from supports without assistance can be highly stressful on the rotator cuff of the shoulder, so it not the optimal way to lift.

Another criticism of the bench press is that it is hard on the shoulders if performed too frequently. During the bench press the shoulder blades are not allowed to move freely because they are pinned against the bench. If an athlete bench-presses three or more times a week and performs a high number of sets, this unnatural motion may result in overuse injuries over time. Benching three times per week will often lead to overtraining and overuse injuries, which is a major problem with many athletes who lift weights. Through doing many clinics and talking to many coaches and athletes, we became aware of the problem of bench press shoulder (more commonly called *rotator cuff tendonitis*). We estimate that 75 percent of all athletes who bench-press three times per week have it.

Bench press shoulder is a dull to sharp pain in the front shoulder joint where the upper arm, chest, and shoulder meet. This pain comes from working out too often with too much weight. Typically, an athlete with this problem has been doing benches three times a week with maximum or near-maximum poundage. The real stress to the shoulder joint comes when the bar is 1 or 2 inches (3-5 centimeters) from the chest. Stretching and putting stress on the shoulder joint three times a week with maximum poundage is bound to cause problems.

The potential for bench press shoulder is one reason this lift is performed only once a week in the Bigger Faster Stronger (BFS) program. If additional work on these muscles groups is desired, then we recommend that the exercise be performed on another workout day through a limited range of motion in the form of a towel bench press.

PRELIFT TECHNIQUE

Proper body position and hand spacing are important when performing the bench press to avoid injuries and get the most strength training benefits.

- **Body Position.** Having proper position during the bench press is extremely important in preventing injuries and being able to get the most strength training effects from the exercise.

Start with your body positioned so that the barbell is directly over your eyes. This position provides enough clearance to prevent the bar from hitting the uprights or safety catches as you perform the lift. Spread your legs wide, which will give you more stability, and place your feet flat on the floor and under the knees. A common fault of novice lifters is lifting the feet off the floor during the bench press, which destroys the firm foundation necessary for maximum effort.

Next, place your hands on the support standards and push your shoulders down toward your hips. A slight arch should be present in the lower back, with your chest sticking up as high as possible. Although this position may be a little uncomfortable at first, it gives the best mechanical advantage and reduces the possibility that you will lift your hips off the bench.

- **Hand Spacing.** The spacing of the hands affects the position of the elbows, which in turn affects the muscles the exercise will develop. A wider grip moves the elbows away from the body and places more emphasis on the chest (figure 9.1a). With this grip the elbows should be at a right angle when the bar is touching the chest. A close grip forces the elbows in, placing more emphasis on the triceps (figure 9.1b).

FIGURE 9.1 A wide (a) and narrow (b) bench press grip.

Most champion bench-pressers and competitive powerlifters use a wide grip. But few sports, even football and wrestling, involve use of the arms in a wide position. A football player, for example, uses the arms with the elbows in close. Therefore, a narrower grip with the elbows in on the bench press simulates the actions that a defensive lineman, linebacker, or bottom-positioned wrestler uses. In 1979, the Pittsburgh Steelers had a group of defensive linemen who could all bench-press 450 pounds (204 kilograms) or more with a narrow, elbows-in grip. (Note that on reaching the halfway point of a narrow-grip bench press, the lifter may force the elbows out for a stronger lockout.)

LIFT TECHNIQUE

Similar to the parallel squat, the bench has four main phases: the start, the descent, the pause on the chest, and the upward drive (figure 9.2 *a-c*). You must concentrate on perfect technique during all parts of the bench press to achieve maximum results.

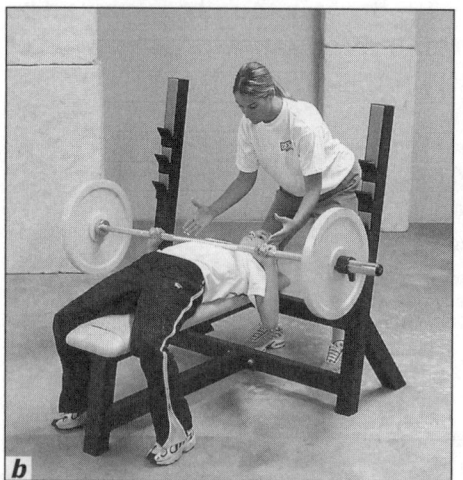

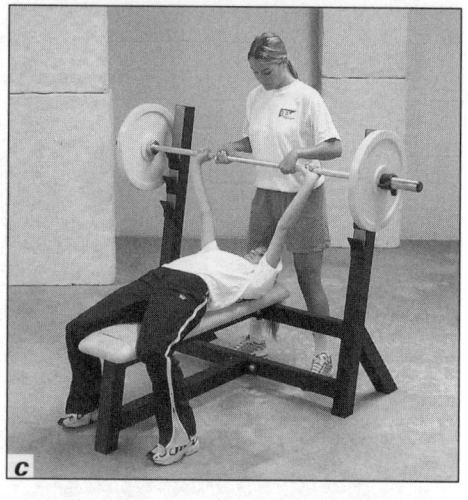

FIGURE 9.2 Proper lift technique and spotting position for the bench press when starting the lift *(a)*, with the bar down on the chest *(b)*, and when the spotter helps the lifter return the bar to the rack *(c)*.

- **Start.** Have a spotter help you lift the weight so that it is positioned directly above your throat. The spotter should not remove the hands from the barbell until the athlete has secured the weight on extended arms and the barbell is motionless.
- **Descent.** Take a deep breath, hold it, and then lower the barbell in an even, controlled manner toward the lower portion of the sternum. (Women will find they have to lower the barbell slightly lower from the sternum than men.)
- **Pause on the chest.** When using a closer grip, the elbows will be pointed more directly to the side than when using a wider grip. Always spread the chest, lock in the lower back, and look at your target.
- **Upward drive.** Press the barbell upward and slightly back, toward the throat. Continue holding your breath when beginning the upward drive from the pause position and then exhale as the barbell passes the hardest position of the lift, or the sticking point. Your eyes should remain fixed on the barbell throughout the entire upward drive. When you complete the set, the spotter should grasp the barbell and help you return it to the supports.

Following are the key points to ensure proper technique for performing the bench press. All of them are important and should continually be reinforced by coaches and teammates.

- **Breathing.** Take a deep breath as the bar comes down. Hold your breath just before the bar touches the chest and up to halfway through the upward movement. At that point you can let the breath out forcefully. Some lifters make loud sounds as they force their breath out. This method keeps everything firm and may have some psychological benefit, especially when performing multiple reps.
- **Squeezing the bar.** Before a max attempt, the technique of squeezing the bar tightly can help, often adding about 5 pounds (2 kilograms) to how much can be lifted. This technique may also reduce stress on the elbows.
- **Angle.** The bar does not go straight down and straight up but rather at a slight angle back toward the rack or the lifter's face. (Competitive powerlifters often use a technique in which the barbell travels straight up and down, but this method should be considered an exception.) As a general guideline, men should lower the barbell to the nipple line, whereas women should lower the barbell to slightly below that level. Finding the correct groove can make a big difference in pounds. Some call this movement a *C curve*.

- **Focus.** If the bar reaches a sticking point, the lifter can sometimes just concentrate on the weaker arm to cause the bar to lock out. Some lifters strain with their eyes closed, which is a mistake. The eyes should always be open and focused on a point directly overhead.

SPOTTING

Most weight training accidents occur at home without a spotter. As a general guideline, a spotter in the middle can provide a more even liftoff and more control over the spot. With heavier weight, such as 300 pounds (136 kilograms), two spotters should be used for the liftoff.

Because working out in groups of three or four is preferred anyway, it doesn't hurt to have everyone involved in spotting. The principal spotter assists the lifter from behind at the middle of the bar and lifts the bar from the standards to the lifter. The principal spotter helps the lifter through the sticking point if the athlete has trouble with the weight. The two side spotters should be on opposite ends of the bar. They touch the bar only when the principal spotter calls for help or when the lifter can't lift the bar from the chest.

COMMON TECHNIQUE PROBLEMS AND SOLUTIONS

Many competitive powerlifters place their thumbs behind the barbell because this positions the lower arm directly below the barbell, providing better leverage and reducing stress on the wrist. The bench press is the most dangerous lift in the weight room. For this reason, we recommend placing the thumbs around the bar. Doing otherwise presents too much risk that the bar will slip and drop on the throat or face. We know 10 lifters who have died bench-pressing. Many lifters have suffered crushed throats, flattened chins, torn lips, lost teeth, smashed noses, torn eyebrows, loss of sight, scalped hair, and smashed foreheads.

VARIATIONS

Athletes should perform two bench workouts per week year-round. One of the workouts should be intense, and the other should be a variation of the bench press. Variations of the bench press, such as dips and combinations of wide and close grips, will help athletes achieve new personal records, month after month.

Towel Bench Press

Our number one choice for the second workout is the towel bench press because it increases confidence and helps prevent pain or injury to the shoulder joint. For this variation, the athlete places a thick, round cushion (a BFS towel bench pad is 5 inches [13 centimeters] in diameter) under the shirt to prevent the barbell from touching the chest. If a towel bench pad is not available, the athlete can make one with three towels rolled up to about a 5-inch (13-centimeter) diameter. The problem with this approach is getting a consistent thickness of the padding.

One of the great benefits of the towel bench press is that it enables athletes to become accustomed to a heavier weight. Normally, on the towel bench athletes can use a weight 10 to 20 pounds (5-9 kilograms) heavier than what they use on the regular bench press. Being successful with the heavier weight builds confidence for attaining new levels on the regular bench.

To perform a towel bench, place the towel bench pad under your shirt. If you don't have a towel bench pad, take three towels and fold them in half the long way. Place them on top of each other and roll them up like a sleeping bag. Lay the rolled-up towels on your chest and then bench with normal technique (figure 9.3*a-b*). Bring the bar right into the pad with more than just a light touch and then drive up.

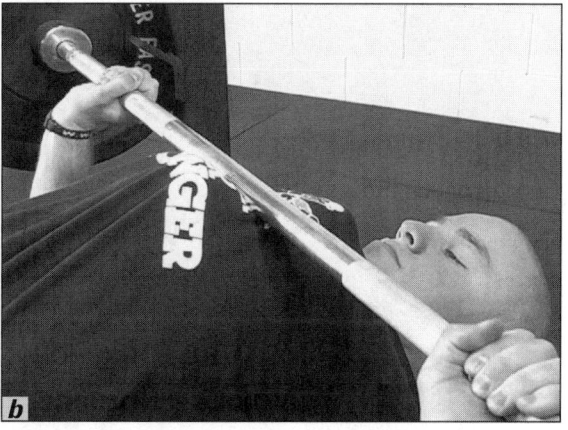

FIGURE 9.3 The towel bench press is performed with a towel or bench pad resting on top of the chest *(a)* or under the shirt *(b)*.

Incline Bench Press

The incline bench press places more emphasis on the shoulders, and the angle from which you press is more specific to many sport movements than the bench press is. Because the pectoral muscles are not as involved, you will lift less than you can with a flat bench press. As a general guideline, the angle of the bench should be 45 degrees, making it halfway between a military press and a bench press. Depending on your sport, you may want to use other angles.

To perform the incline bench press, lie face up on an incline bench press station. For greatest stability, spread your legs slightly wider than shoulder width apart and place your feet flat on the floor. As with the regular bench press, grasp the barbell with a shoulder-width grip and have a spotter help you position the weight at arm's length directly above your throat (figure 9.4).

Lower the weight to the upper portion of your pectorals, creating the shortest distance for the bar to travel. As you lower the weight, your elbows should point slightly down, not directly out to the sides. Without bouncing the barbell off your chest, press the weight back to the start, with the barbell traveling in a slight arch backward. At first this

FIGURE 9.4 The incline bench press places more emphasis on the shoulders.

action may feel awkward, because the natural tendency is to press the barbell forward, but you'll quickly master the technique. When you've completed all the reps for a set, have your spotter help guide the barbell back to the supports. Breathe using the same technique you used with the flat bench press.

LIFTING CHAINS

Although widespread use of chains for weight training is a recent practice, chains have been around since the early days of modern resistance training, and over 40 years ago Nautilus inventor Arthur Jones wrote about experimenting with lifting chains. Jones didn't pursue chains, deciding instead to use a shell-shaped cam to vary resistance on his machines.

Lifting chains can be used in the bench press and all its variations. Applying the concept of variable resistance, lifting chains gradually make the bar heavier as you lift the weight. Your muscles therefore work as hard as possible during the entire lift (see figure 9.5).

Normally, adding about 10 percent at the finish position of the lift is most beneficial. We recommend three chains: a varsity chain that adds about 15 pounds (7 kilograms) to a bench press, an all-state chain that adds about 25 pounds (11 kilograms) to a bench press, and an all-American chain that adds about 55 pounds (25 kilograms) to a squat

FIGURE 9.5 Using lifting chains gradually makes the bar heavier as you lift the weight causing the lift to match the athlete's strength curve.

and 37 pounds (17 kilograms) to a bench press. Here are more specific guidelines:

- **Varsity chain.** This chain is for athletes who bench less than 200 pounds (91 kilograms) and squat with less than 300 pounds (136 kilograms).
- **All-state chain.** Athletes who bench between 200 and 300 pounds (91 and 136 kilograms) and squat between 300 and 400 pounds (136 and 181 kilograms) use this chain.
- **All-American chain.** This chain is for athletes who bench over 300 pounds (136 kilograms) and squat over 400 pounds (181 kilograms). Two chains will fit easily on each side of the bar, which allows different combinations to be created. By putting the all-state and all-American chains on together, you can add 62 pounds (28 kilograms) on the bench and 95 pounds (43 kilograms) on the squat.

You should record what is on the bar plus the code of whatever chain you are using. Use *VC* for the varsity chain, *AS* for the all-state chain, and *AA* for the all-American chain. For example, an athlete who does 185 pounds (84 kilograms) plus the varsity chain would record "185 VC."

Lifting chains can make a difference. Have fun with them and get new maxes quicker than ever before!

CHAPTER 10

Sport-Specific Auxiliary Lifts

Auxiliary lifts are special exercises that are sport specific and help prevent common injuries common in a sport. Because the latissimus dorsi muscles of the upper back internally rotate the upper arms, lat pull-downs would be a sport-specific exercise for baseball players. And neck exercises are extremely important to prevent injuries in football and wrestling, but they are not that important to basketball or baseball players.

Auxiliary exercises receive less emphasis than core lifts. They are best performed after the core lifts and are generally only prescribed for about two sets of 10 reps. Larger groups may find it necessary to rotate athletes between core lifts and auxiliaries as outlined in chapter 15, Organization and Weight Room Design.

Select no more than five auxiliary exercises. Performing more than five auxiliary exercises will cause problems because athletes will not have enough time and energy to do the necessary sprinting, stamina, flexibility, plyometric, agility, and technique work required for their sport. Remember, the ultimate objective is for athletes to reach their potential. Therefore, select only those exercises that will effectively contribute to the ultimate objective.

Which auxiliary exercises are best? Our Bigger Faster Stronger (BFS) clinicians rated 100 auxiliary lifts and came up with a list of preferred exercises. We have divided these auxiliary lifts into two categories—standard and advanced.

STANDARD AUXILIARY LIFTS

Standard auxiliary exercises are relatively safe, are easy to perform, and require less coaching and lifting expertise than the advanced auxiliaries. The incline press is the only auxiliary that requires a spotter. Of course, coaches and athletes must be careful teaching and supervising all of them.

Most high school and college gyms already have all the equipment necessary to implement these exercises. One exception is the glute–ham machine or back extension bench, which some gyms might not own but which should be a top priority for auxiliary exercises. The glute–ham raise is also among the BFS advanced auxiliaries. Table 10.1 shows how to organize the standard auxiliary exercises in your weekly training sessions. Table 10.2 lists all the auxiliary exercises and the sports for which they are the most appropriate.

Table 10.1 Weekly Auxiliary Lifting Schedule

Monday	Wednesday	Friday
Neck exercise	Lat pull	Neck exercise
Leg curl	Heavy dips	Leg curl
Leg extension	Incline press	Leg extension
Glute–ham raise	Shoulder press	Glute–ham raise
Straight-leg deadlift	Lunge	Straight-leg deadlift

Dips

Although seldom performed today, dips are a great exercise to develop the shoulders, pectorals, and triceps (figure 10.1).

Start position: Grasp the dip handles and step up so that your arms are extended and directly under your shoulders. Look straight ahead.

Action: Slowly lower yourself so that your arms extend below parallel and then return to the start. As this exercise becomes easy, you will be able to add resistance by using a dip belt.

Breathing: Inhale as you lower your body and exhale as you straighten your arms.

FIGURE 10.1 Dips develop powerful triceps.

Glute–Ham Raise

A BFS favorite, the glute–ham raise is the only exercise that develops both the hip extension and knee flexion functions of the hamstrings (figure 10.2).

Start position: Lie facedown on a back extension bench or glute–ham developer, adjusting the hip pad so that your hip bones extend slightly over the edge of the bench. Hook your ankles under the roller pad and place your hands across your chest or behind your head. As you get stronger, you can hold weights across your chest.

Action: Keeping your head aligned with your

FIGURE 10.2 The glute–ham raise helps prevent hamstring pulls.

Table 10.2   Auxiliary Exercises for Specific Sports

	BB	BK	CH	FB	FH	GF	GYM	HK
Standard auxiliary lifts								
Dips	X	X	X	X			X	
Incline bench press	X					X		
Lat pull-down			X		X		X	X
Leg curl		X				X		
Leg extension								
Leg press								X
Dumbbell lunge	X	X	X	X	X		X	X
Neck exercise				X		X		
Shoulder press	X	X	X		X			X
Glute–ham raise	X	X		X	X			X
Straight-leg deadlift	X	X	X	X			X	
Advanced auxiliary lifts*								
Power snatch						X		
Push jerk			X				X	
Push press				X				

■ **LEGEND**   BB: Baseball, SK/SB: Skiing/Snowboarding, BK: Basketball, SOC: Soccer, CH: Cheerleading, SB: Softball, FB: Football, SW: Swimming, FH: Field hockey, TN: Tennis, GF: Golf, TK: Track, GYM: Gymnastics, VB: Volleyball, HK: Hockey, WR: Wrestling, LAC: Lacrosse, XC: Cross country, RUG: Rugby

*Power balance drills could be used for all sports, especially as a warm-up.
The straight-leg deadlift and the glute–ham raise are appropriate for all sports.

LAC	RUG	SK/SB	SOC	SB	SW	TN	TK	VB	WR	XC
				X	X	X	X		X	
	X						X		X	
X		X			X	X		X	X	X
		X	X				X			X
		X	X		X		X			
		X								
X	X		X			X	X	X		X
	X								X	
X				X	X			X		
		X	X		X				X	
			X			X				
X				X		X		X		
					X					
	X									

spine, lift your torso until your back is parallel to the floor. Continue the movement by bending your knees to lift your torso higher. Reverse the technique to return to the start.

Breathing: Holding your breath, raise your torso all the way up. Exhale halfway down or at the finish.

Incline Bench Press

This variation of the bench press places more emphasis on the shoulders and less on the pectorals. Always use a spotter when performing this exercise (figure 10.3).

Start position: Lie face up on the incline bench press station and spread your legs shoulder width apart, feet flat on the floor. Grasp the barbell with an overhand, shoulder-width grip. Have a spotter help you lift the weight to arm's length.

Action: Lower the weight to your upper chest. As you lower the weight, your elbows should point slightly down, not flared out at your sides. When the bar touches your chest, press the weight back to the start. When you've finished your set, have your spotter help guide the barbell back to the supports.

Breathing: Hold your breath, lower the bar, and exhale as you press the weight and after you've passed the sticking point.

FIGURE 10.3 The incline bench press.

Lat Pull-Down

Lat pull-downs work the major muscles of the upper back, especially the latissimus dorsi and the biceps. The standard exercise requires a lat pull-down machine with a straight bar (figure 10.4), but many variations can be performed with different grip handles. For example, a V-handle allows you to perform the exercise with a close, parallel grip.

Start position: Grasp the straight bar with an overhand grip, spreading your hands slightly wider than shoulder width apart. Sit on the bench, facing the weight stack, with your legs positioned under the thigh pad. Look straight ahead.

Action: Pull the bar to your upper chest, leaning slightly back as you do so; when the bar touches your chest, your shoulder blades should be pinched together. Return the bar to the start.

Breathing: Exhale as you pull the bar toward your chest; inhale as you return it to the start position.

FIGURE 10.4 The lat pull-down can be done using various grips. Here it is done with a wide grip in front of the neck.

Leg Curl

The leg curl machine isolates the knee flexion function of the hamstrings. Rather than a flat bench, many equipment manufacturers offer a V-bench design that minimizes hyperextension of the lower back, which is valuable because many people find hyperextension uncomfortable (figure 10.5).

FIGURE 10.5 Leg curls develop the hamstrings.

Start position: Position your body on the machine so your ankles rest behind the pads and your knees are in line with the center of the pulley.

Action: Flex your knees and pull the ankle pad toward your buttocks, and then return to the start. Perform the exercise slowly—do not jerk the weight. If you cannot achieve a full range of motion during this exercise, the weight is probably too heavy or your knees are not in line with the pulley.

Breathing: Hold your breath, bend your knees, and exhale during the descent.

Leg Extension

This popular leg exercise develops the quadriceps and is often used in knee rehabilitation (figure 10.6).

Start position: Position yourself on a leg extension machine and grasp the handles to steady your torso. You should be positioned so that the pads are directly behind or in front of your ankles; placing them over the top of the foot places excessive pressure on the shins and knees.

Action: Raise the ankle pads until your knees are straight. Slowly lower the weight to return to the start position.

Breathing: Exhale as you lift the weight and inhale as you lower it.

FIGURE 10.6 Leg extensions develop the quadriceps and strengthen the knee joints.

Leg Press

The leg press is a particularly effective exercise because it works all the major lower-body muscles through an extensive range of motion. The leg press machine supports the lower back, which is valuable for athletes who have injuries that prevent them from squatting (figure 10.7).

Start position: Position yourself in the machine so your feet are flat on the footplate and your back and shoulders are in contact with the backrest. Grasp the handles. Straighten your legs until they are straight but not hyperextended, and turn the safety catch so the weight can slide freely.

Action: Lower the weight as far as comfortable, being careful to avoid lowering the weight so far that you round the lower back. If this is not possible, then you are probably using too much weight. When you've lowered the footplate to an appropriate position, extend your legs to return it to the start. When you've completed all the reps for that set, turn the safety catch to secure the weight.

FIGURE 10.7 The leg press is effective because it works all of the major muscles of the lower body through an extensive range of motion.

Breathing: Hold your breath, bend your knees, and exhale as you press the weight after you're past the sticking point.

Lunge

The lunge is a simple exercise that develops the quadriceps and hamstrings throughout a full range of motion. Because it takes some practice to become proficient holding a barbell for the lunge, this is a great exercise to help beginners learn proper form (figure 10.8).

Start position: Grasp a dumbbell in each hand so that your palms are facing each other and spread your feet about hip width apart. Hold your chest up, shoulders back, and head facing forward.

Action: Take a step forward and lower your hips, allowing the trailing knee to lower to a point just before

FIGURE 10.8 The lunge can be done with or without dumbbells.

it touches the floor. Push off with the forward leg and then step back to return to the start. Repeat this movement for the opposite leg. One repetition consists of a lunge with each leg.

Breathing: Hold your breath, lunge forward, and exhale during the ascent after you're past the sticking point.

Neck Exercise

Training the muscles of the neck helps prevent serious injuries in sports such as football, wrestling, and soccer (figure 10.9).

Start position: The neck machine allows four exercises to work the flexion, extension, and lateral flexion of the next muscles. As such, you will face four different directions when performing all the exercises on this machine.

Action: Depending on how you are sitting, you will flex, extend, or laterally flex your neck to work the specific muscles that perform these functions. Perform all exercises slowly, and do not jerk the weight.

FIGURE 10.9 Neck exercise performed on a seated neck machine.

Breathing: Exhale as you start each movement and inhale as you return to the start.

Shoulder Press

The shoulder press, or military press, is a great exercise for the shoulders and triceps (figure 10.10). It can be performed standing or seated.

Start position: Grasp a barbell with an overhand grip, hands about shoulder width apart. Rest the barbell on your shoulders.

Action: Press the barbell overhead to arm's length and then lower to the start. Do not lean backward at any point during the exercise; this can injure the lower back.

Breathing: Hold your breath, press the barbell overhead, and exhale after you've pressed the weights to straight arm's length. Inhale as you lower the weight.

FIGURE 10.10 Shoulder presses can be performed seated, standing, and with dumbbells.

Straight-Leg Deadlift

This is a great exercise for increasing flexibility in the hamstrings and strengthening the lower back (figure 10.11).

Start position: Stand in front of the barbell and position your feet about hip width apart. Crouch down and grasp the barbell, and then stand up so the barbell is resting on your mid-thighs.

Action: Lower the barbell as far as comfortable, keeping the barbell close to your body throughout the exercise. Continue leaning forward as far as comfortable, and then return to the start. As your flexibility improves, you will eventually be able to perform this exercise while standing on a low platform.

Breathing: Inhale as you lower the weight and exhale as you lift it.

FIGURE 10.11 The straight-leg deadlift stretches the hamstrings and strengthens the lower back.

ADVANCED AUXILIARY LIFTS

The advanced auxiliary lifts are harder to perform than the standard auxiliaries and require more coaching and organization. Any overhead lift is considered an advanced lift. Coaches should use caution before giving the green light for larger groups. Only after learning the basic lifting techniques and thoroughly understanding the six absolutes (see chapter 5) will athletes benefit from these exercises. Also, because of their complexity, they should only be performed for five reps or less.

Push Jerk

This great shoulder exercise will also help develop power in the legs. Place the barbell behind the neck in a high-bar squat position, squat down slightly, and thrust the bar explosively upward. As you do this, quickly spread your feet apart as you would when doing an Olympic-style clean and jerk. The bar will end up overhead in a locked position, at which point you stand upright to complete the lift (figure 10.12). Push jerks develop upper-body explosiveness and shoulder strength. You can also perform this exercise with the barbell resting on the front of the shoulders using the starting position of the shoulder press.

FIGURE 10.12 The push jerk.

Power Snatch

The power snatch (figure 10.13a-d) is a tremendous lift for any athlete to develop overall power. Many athletes find this exercise easier on the wrists than the power clean. If you can perform a power clean with good technique, you might want to try a power snatch. You can even use the power snatch as a core lift, substituting it for the power clean. The proper technique for performing the power snatch is provided in chapter 7 on pages 87-89.

FIGURE 10.13 The power snatch *(a-d)* is a great lift for any athlete to develop overall power. Start the pull with your legs and hips and keep the bar close to your body *(a-b)*. As you finish the pull keep the elbows high *(c)* and snap explosively into catch position *(d)*.

Push Press

Assume the position you used for the jerk and squat down slightly. Thrust the bar upward explosively with the legs and arms. Then explosively pop your feet out from your jump stance into a high squat position as you would in a power clean (figure 10.14).

FIGURE 10.14 The push press.

POWER BALANCE DRILLS

You can perform these challenging and entertaining drills in tandem with the power snatch. The neat thing about our balance drills is that they can challenge even a strong athlete using only the bar.

When balance comes into play during exercise, the body uses many muscles. This factor is one of the primary reasons why athletes choose free weights over machines. For example, the prime movers in a standing curl are the biceps, but were it not for the stabilizing muscles in the back and hips, the lifter would fall over. Athletes stride out a long way during lunges, thereby learning to balance themselves powerfully in an awkward position, a position that is often duplicated in athletic competition. When an exercise uses the stabilizing muscles as much as the prime movers, it is a power balance exercise.

Tom Cross, who has been a strength coach at MidAmerica Nazarene University, caused us to think about some additional power balance lifts several years ago. As a result, we began including three of them during the auxiliary lift presentation at BFS clinics. Before we give this lift presentation, the athletes and coaches have experienced a thorough practical introduction to the six absolutes of coaching and have worked on the power clean for about an hour. During the power clean presentation, all athletes have experienced a front squat from a power clean position. The final lift presented at a BFS clinic before we discuss the three power balance lifts is the power snatch. All athletes should go through the same experience before trying the following three power balance lifts.

Power Balance Drill 1

Perform a power snatch and stand erect in an athletic stance. Now squat all the way down while maintaining balance and proper technique. Hold the low position for three seconds and then stand erect again (figure 10.15a-b).

FIGURE 10.15 Power balance drill 1. Start position *(a)* and low position *(b)*.

Power Balance Drill 2

Place the bar on your shoulders as if you are going to do a back squat while using a snatch grip. Again, squat all the way down and balance yourself. Then see if you can press the weight all the way up. The challenge is to see if you can press the bar up from your shoulders while maintaining perfect balance (figure 10.16a-b).

FIGURE 10.16 Power balance drill 2. Start position *(a)* and with the weight pressed up *(b)*.

Power Balance Drill 3

Do power balance drill 2, but this time see if you can press it up, hold it for three seconds, and then stand erect.

Variation helps keep athletes motivated so that they continue to train hard and break records. Coaches should have their athletes focus on the core lifts but use the auxiliary lifts to ensure a greater commitment to success.

Kiley Allosso:
2007 BFS Female High School Athlete of the Year

When she was 5 years old, Kiley Allosso had an unusual request for Santa Claus: She wanted a field hockey stick. Although Kiley had never played the game—there aren't many youth field hockey leagues for 5-year-olds—she knew that there was something special about being a field hockey player in her hometown.

If there were a mythical Narnia of girls field hockey, it would be Frank Cox High School in Virginia Beach. The Falcons have won 14 state championships and are beloved by both the student body and the community. Kiley wanted to be a part of this experience, which she did quickly by making the varsity field hockey squad as a freshman. In 2007, Kiley, considered a team leader by her field hockey coach Julie Swain, saw the Falcons go undefeated, winning 23 straight games.

Part of Kiley Allosso's success comes from her regimen of BFS auxiliary lifts.

Kiley's success in field hockey is just one of many reasons she was selected as the 2007 BFS Female High School Athlete of the Year. Kiley is a multisport athlete who also excels in soccer and basketball. Kiley is also an outstanding student, carrying a near-perfect 3.933 grade point average, and is active in charitable endeavors and works with the preschool program at her church. And there's one more thing—Kiley, who stands 5 feet, 7 inches (170 centimeters), is physically very strong. Just how strong is Kiley? Consider these lifts: power clean, 150 pounds (68 kilograms); bench press, 130 pounds (59 kilograms); parallel squat, 235 pounds (107 kilograms); and hex-bar deadlift, 260 pounds (118 kilograms).

Kiley's father, Steve, is the head football coach at Frank Cox High School and oversees the weight program. Considering Kiley's love for sports, and because Steve wanted to give his daughter every opportunity for success, he encouraged Kiley to start the BFS readiness program in seventh grade. Asked if she had concerns about getting muscle-bound, Kiley replies, "Since I was in seventh grade I didn't care, and I really wanted to be stronger than my opponents and even stronger than some of the boys in my class."

> continued

> *continued*

As much as she loved sports, she loved lifting hard and breaking records. Steve recalls that after one practice, Kiley begged him to open the weight room for her at 9 p.m. "Kiley said, 'I know I can break eight records today,' but she only broke four and came home very upset. My wife asked, 'What did you say to her—what did you do?' I said, 'I didn't do anything; she was just upset because she only broke four personal records.' That's shows you how much importance she puts on her weight training program."

Swain has seen this attitude in action. "Kiley is constantly working hard to improve and is so easy to coach. She has a tremendous work ethic, is a great leader by example, and is always, always, a competitor."

Kiley is determined to make the U.S. national field hockey team. Why does field hockey mean so much to her? "I'm a competitive person," says Kiley. "I love working out, I love my team, I love my coach, I love everything about the game. And it's always been fun!"

PART III

Speed, Agility, and Flexibility

CHAPTER 11

Agility and the BFS Dot Drill

One of the most complex and controversial topics in strength and conditioning is how to warm up properly. Dynamic exercise, aerobic training, PNF stretching—no wonder so many high school coaches throw up their hands and just say, "Go run a lap!" At Bigger Faster Stronger (BFS), we've found a simple and effective method of properly warming up for lifting. It's called the *dot drill*.

If nothing else, a warm-up needs to increase body temperature, breathing rate, and heart rate to the level of the activity to be performed. This means you need to break a sweat, so static stretching is not what you need—after a workout, yes, but not before.

Certainly running around in circles or spending a few minutes pedaling a stationary bike will heat you up, get your blood pumping, and make you breathe hard, but does this sound like the type of warm-up an athlete should use? Instead, we prefer that athletes use the dot drill to warm up before all workouts.

The dot drill is an ideal warm-up because not only does it fulfill all the requirements of a good warm-up, but it improves coordination, foot speed, and agility as well. It also strengthens the ankles, which could be considered a weak link in the body because they are frequently injured in athletics and can be frustrating to rehabilitate. And because an athlete who injures an ankle is five times more likely to injure it again, it makes sense to include exercises that will prevent the ankles from becoming injured in the first place.

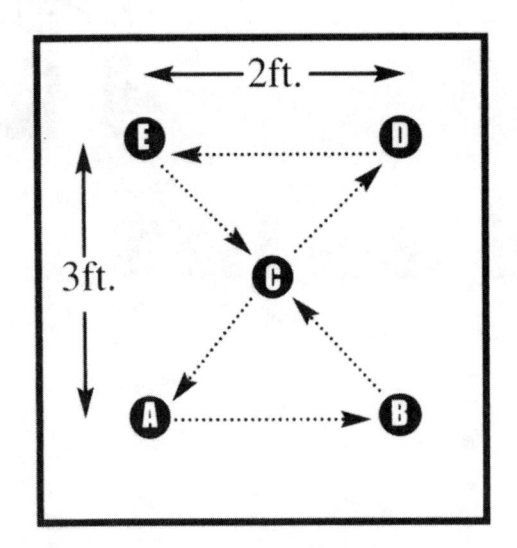

Place five dots on the floor (figure 11.1). The drill works best with 4-inch (10-centimeter) dots painted on the floor. Some coaches paint many stations for larger groups. At home, athletes can use anything approved by their parents to mark the dots. There are five components to the dot drill, and the components are performed six times.

FIGURE 11.1 The dot drill.

Drill 1: Up and Back

1. Start at one end with feet on A and B (left foot on A, right foot on B).
2. Jump quickly with both feet to C, then with split feet to D and E.
3. Come back the same way, without turning around.
4. Repeat five times.

Drill 2: Right Foot

1. After doing the up-and-back drill, your feet should be on A and B. Now jump to C with only your right foot.
2. Using only the right foot, go in order from D to E to C to A to B.
3. Repeat five times.

Drill 3: Left Foot

1. The right-foot drill ends with the feet on B. Now go to C with your left foot.
2. Using only the left foot, go in order from D to E to C to A to B.
3. Repeat five times.

Drill 4: Both Feet

1. The left-foot drill ends with the feet on B. Now go to C with both feet.

2. With both feet, go in order from D to E to C to A to B.
3. Repeat five times.

Drill 5: Turn Around

1. The both-feet drill ends with the feet on B. Now go to C with both feet.
2. Go to D and E with split feet, as in the up-and-back drill.
3. Quickly jump and turn 180 degrees to the right and face the other way. You should still be on D and E.
4. Hit C with both feet and then A and B with split feet.
5. Turn quickly again, spinning 180 degrees to the left with split feet still on A and B.
6. Repeat five times.

Note that you will be facing the same direction on all the drills except the turn-around drill. A simple phrase to remember when performing the right-foot, left-foot, and both-feet drills is "in, out, across":

In to the middle (to C)

Out to D

Across to E

In to the middle (to C)

Out to A

Across to B

When athletes first attempt the dot drill, they often feel clumsy and find it extremely tiring. But these difficulties will pass, especially if the athlete commits to performing the drill six times a week. That may seem like a big commitment, but consider that the record for the dot drill is 33.37 seconds for boys and 37.77 seconds for girls. For most athletes, we're asking for less than 10 minutes of work per week—an investment well worth the price. And it's easy to have the whole team run the drill at the same time (figure 11.2).

At BFS, we've found that if you're really serious about improving performance in any aspect of strength and conditioning, you have to test it. Whether it's by how much you lift, how high you jump, or how fast you run, you have to find a way to accurately measure performance so you can set personal records and then break those records. This is also true with the dot drill, and we recommend that athletes test themselves twice a month and record the results.

FIGURE 11.2 The entire team can easily perform dot drill at the same time.

To help athletes determine how they are doing on the dot drill, BFS has established a set of standards for both female and male athletes. Table 11.1 shows these standards. We believe the BFS dot drill is a perfect warm-up for any athlete at any age. There are many more ways to prepare the body for a workout, but for its simplicity and effectiveness, you can't beat the BFS dot drill.

Table 11.1 BFS Dot Drill Standards for Males and Females

Grade	Males	Females
All-American	Under 40 sec	Under 45 sec
Super quick	40-49 sec	45-54 sec
Great	50-59 sec	55-64 sec
Average	60-70 sec	65-75 sec
Needs more work	Over 70 sec	Over 75 sec

BFS dot drill records:
High school boys record: Michael Brown 33.37, Poplar Bluff, Missouri
High school girls record: Kristian Meyers 37.77 sec, Poplar Bluff, Missouri

Cat Scratch Fever at Deer Park High

A great strength and conditioning program is a must for championship football teams like Deer Park High.

Many high school football players dream of one day playing professional football. Others dream of becoming coaches so they can continue enjoying the thrills of Friday night lights. And in a perfect world, wouldn't it be great to come back and coach at the school you graduated from? In Cincinnati, Ohio, there's a coach who is doing just that.

Welcome to the world of Barry Pettyjohn and the Wildcats of Deer Park High School. Pettyjohn has been the head coach at Deer Park, a Class 2A school, for the past five years. He graduated from the school in 1982, and after college ball in Pittsburgh, he played the offensive line for the Houston Oilers in 1987 and for the Miami Dolphins for the following two years. With such impressive qualifications, it may be a surprise that he decided to return to his alma mater. After all, the Deer Park Wildcats were not so wild on the football field. The team hadn't had a winning season since 1999, and the last time the team was in the play-offs, it was Pettyjohn's senior year!

In his first year as head coach, Pettyjohn managed to coach his team to a 5-5 record. The next year it was back to their losing ways—they lost every single game, and they managed only two wins the following year. Says Pettyjohn, "I think part of the problem was not always getting the best quality of kids to come out for the team, but most of all it was that the kids lacked confidence in themselves. When we went 0-10, you could see their confidence falling, and the next year we had kids playing who had never won a varsity game, and that's why we went 2-8. That's when I said that was enough and that we needed to get these kids confidence—and the best way to get confidence is in the weight room."

"When I came in, we were lifting weights and we had a pretty good strength program going, but although they were good kids, they didn't work as hard as they could," says Pettyjohn. "I had been a part of a lot of different weight lifting programs, but I found out that in working with kids it's not what I believe in, it's what the kids believe in." So he started searching for a better strength training program.

> continued

> *continued*

Having heard good things about BFS, Pettyjohn attended a clinic in Beaver Creek, Ohio, and after that experience he'd made up his mind on what path to take. "I was sold on the BFS concept about how you can get the maximum amount of work done and increase your strength in a minimum amount of time. It made sense to me, and I bought into it and so did my athletic director. Then we had a meeting with the parents and showed them the DVD that Dr. Shepard had made overviewing the program, and they bought into it." Pettyjohn purchased the BFS Beat the Computer program and set up times for the athletes to lift before and after school. A boost in their confidence was only the beginning.

"When we were 0-10, that year we didn't have one person who could bench over 250 pounds [113 kilograms], and I don't know if we had anyone who could squat over 300 [136 kilograms]. This year we had eight kids bench over 250, and there were kids box squatting 450 [204 kilograms] and even 500 [227 kilograms]. The gains in the weight room are unbelievable."

In addition to implementing BFS' simple approach to conditioning, Pettyjohn applied that philosophy to his on-field coaching. He says, "If you keep things simple, then there is no confusion. I think sometimes as coaches we have egos and we want to show how many different plays we know, how many defense schemes we know, how many different kickoffs we know, and we confuse the kids. And it's not what the coach knows; it's what the kids know. So although we run a lot of different formations, we run six or seven different plays out of them. Coaches know a lot of things in their head about how to play the game, but no coaches play the game. What matters is what the athlete knows so that he can play the game fast. That's the biggest thing—you have to play football fast."

In 2006, the Wildcats had a simple motto: "Play to win!" And win they did, scoring eight victories, their last one against a team they hadn't beaten in 18 years, and making it to the play-offs. "Everyone at the school and in the community was so excited—they called what was happening 'cat scratch fever,' and for the first time it was cool to wear a Deer Park football shirt. We even had a bonfire before the state play-off game, and whereas we usually get 1,000 people at a game, for the play-offs we had more than 3,000!"

Although they fell short of their ultimate goal of winning the state championships in 2007, the Wildcats of Deer Park High School are already back in the weight room getting ready for next season. They know it won't be easy. "Now other people are gunning for us and saying, 'We want to beat Deer Park this year!'" says Pettyjohn. "But we have a good group of kids coming back who are united and motivated—and they have great confidence!"

CHAPTER 12

Five-Phase Plyometric Program

In most sports, the champions of today are bigger, faster, and stronger than the champions of the past. Athletic performance has reached such a high level that there are high school athletes who could beat the times that won swimmer Mark Spitz seven Olympic gold medals in 1972, and even the great Jesse Owens would have trouble keeping up with the world's top female sprinters.

With such expectations placed on future champions, athletes are seeking new and better ways to fulfill their physical potential. The process begins with a solid readiness program of Bigger Faster Stronger (BFS) core lifts such as the squat and the power clean, as well as low-intensity agility exercises such as the BFS dot drill. But to reach the next level and set new standards of sporting excellence, an athlete should consider engaging in the highest level of performance conditioning, a method called *plyometrics*.

Plyometrics is a key component of the BFS program because it is one of the best ways to improve speed and power, especially for elite athletes. In the United States, the term *plyometrics* describes any activity that involves the rapid stretching of a muscle (eccentric phase) immediately followed by the rapid shortening of that muscle (concentric phase). Thus, a standing broad jump is plyometric because it involves rapid stretching and shortening of the quadriceps muscles.

More specific definitions of plyometrics apply when considering the level of tension involved in the activity. For example, jumping rope would be more accurately called *preparatory plyometrics* because it does not produce a high level of muscle tension, but it helps condition the body and nervous system for more intense forms of plyometrics. The squat would also be considered a form of preparatory plyometrics because although it involves a stretching and shortening of the quadriceps muscles, the speed component is relatively small and doesn't produce the highest levels of muscle tension.

Former world-class discus thrower Stefan Fernholm said that plyometrics played a major role in getting his 40-yard (37-meter) dash time down to 4.3 seconds and his vertical jump to 39 inches (99 centimeters) at a body weight of 270 pounds (123 kilograms). Besides the field data of athletic success stories, considerable peer-reviewed research is available to prove that plyometrics works.

For example, in a paper published in the *Journal of Applied Sports Science Research* in 1992, researchers conducted a six-week study on the effects of squatting and plyometrics on the vertical jump. The group that performed just the squat increased their vertical jump 1.3 inches (3.3 centimeters), a significant improvement for six weeks. When plyometrics was combined with squatting, however, the increase was 4.2 inches (10.7 centimeters)! With scientifically documented improvements of that magnitude, you can see why plyometrics is an integral part of the BFS program.

Frank Costello, in his book *Bounding to the Top*, explains how plyometrics works: "The athlete stores kinetic energy while descending and converts it to potential energy for the concentric contraction required to respond immediately. The myostatic, or stretch, reflex makes this reaction possible." Simply put, plyometric training involves maximum explosive contractions performed as quickly as possible. As such, when performing plyometrics your feet should spend as little time as possible in contact with the ground. When you jump up, you use maximum effort. When you bound for height or distance, you go all out. You are teaching your body how to use its strength. You are going to become explosive!

JUMPING INTO THE PROGRAM

The BFS plyometric program takes just 10 minutes, twice a week—that's it! The first phase of this program is to perform 10 quality vertical jumps. Do the vertical jumps by a wall or basketball standard. Note the height of the first jump and then try to improve with each successive jump. Take a minimum of 15 seconds rest between vertical jumps.

The second phase of the program is to perform three sets of three successive standing long jumps. Both the vertical jump and the standing long jump are easily implemented into any conditioning program because they require no special equipment. To encourage athletes to train hard on these exercises, both the vertical jump and the long jump should be tested once a month.

Plyometric box jumping is the third phase. Assuming that you have the proper plyometric boxes (figures 12.1 and 12.2a-b), begin by performing five jumps from a 20-inch (51-centimeter) box and then land in an athletic stance. Those who have trouble with the 20-inch boxes can use 10-inch (25-centimeter) readiness boxes. Now jump in the

FIGURE 12.1 Various heights of boxes enable athletes of all levels to perform plyometric exercises.

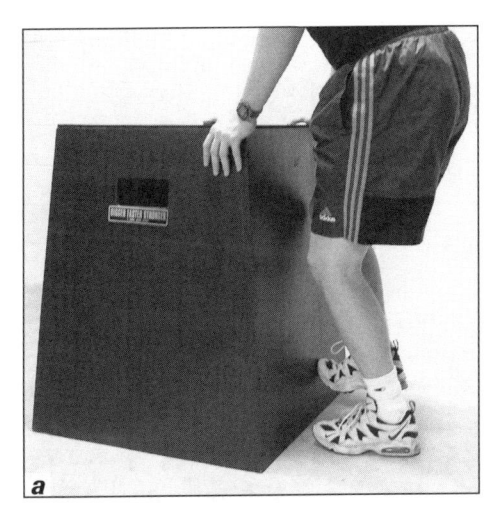

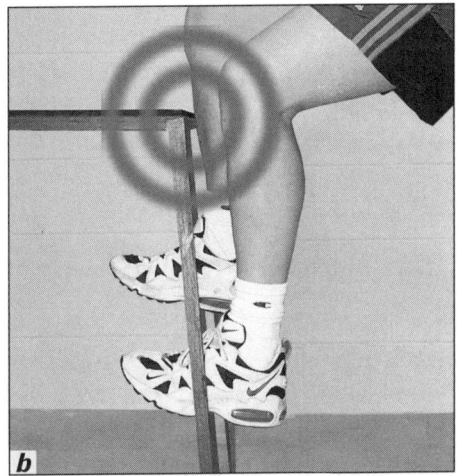

FIGURE 12.2 With a solid plyometric box (a), the foot safely slides down. With an open box (b), the feet can get trapped, causing injury.

same manner, but this time recoil straight up as quickly as possible. On the next series, jump from one box to the floor and then to the next box; repeat five times. Finish the workout by following the same procedure, but complete it as rapidly as possible. You should have four to five boxes, each about 20 inches (51 centimeters) high. As you become more advanced, you can raise the height of the last box. For boys, a good jump for the last box is 36 inches (91 centimeters), and for girls, a good jump is 32 inches (81 centimeters). See figure 12.3*a-d* for various phases of plyometric box jumping.

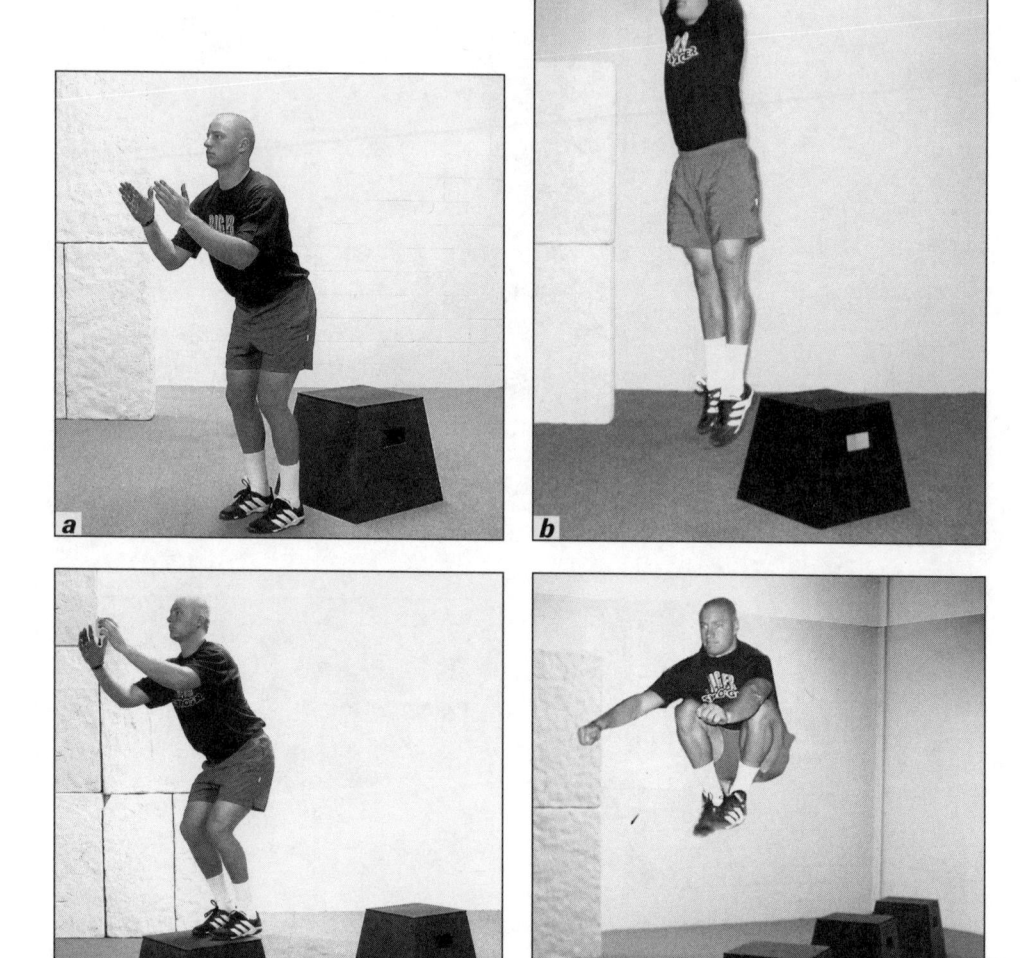

FIGURE 12.3 Various phases of plyometric box jumping: landing on the floor *(a)*, vertical jump *(b)*, landing on the box *(c)*, and multiple box jumps *(d)*.

The fourth phase of the program is to jump on a box from a stand. This phase will create interest and enthusiasm for plyometrics. Coaches may wish to test a standing box jump once a month.

The final phase can be a series of plyometric bounding drills, which, as the accompanying photos show, are running drills in which the leg drive is exaggerated so that more height and distance are covered with each foot contact (figure 12.4*a-d*).

FIGURE 12.4 Plyometric bounding drills. Hurdle jumping *(a)*, side hops *(b)*, bounding for height *(c)*, and bounding for speed *(d)*.

All these phases may sound like a lot to do in just 10 minutes, but you can do it if you are organized. Divide a class into two main groups; one group can work on speed while the other works on plyometrics. Divide the speed group in half, with one group working on technique and the other working on sprints. You can also divide the plyometric group into two groups. Half can be doing bounding, vertical jumps, and standing long jumps while the other half works on box jumping. This training can be tremendously productive and pay great dividends in improved athletic performance.

THE STANDING BOX JUMP

One exercise we implement in the BFS program is the standing box jump. Box jumping for height can be a great part of your plyometric program and total conditioning program.

Box jumping bridges the gap between strength and explosive power. Being able to squat 500 pounds (227 kilograms) is great, but that alone does not ensure explosive power. Box jumping can help the muscular system contract more quickly and with greater force. Box jumping works through a principle similar to the overload principle in weight training. As athletes gradually increase the resistance or the weight on the bar, they become stronger. Likewise, a gradual increase in the height of the plyometric boxes produces an increase in explosive power and jumping ability.

You can measure improvements in jumping ability in several ways. The most common way is to measure an athlete's vertical jump. You can also measure an athlete's standing long jump, either for one jump or for three successive jumps. Another way is to have an athlete jump up onto a box. There are also affordable electronic force platforms that make testing quick and accurate, even allowing you to test single-leg jumps and multiple jumps (see figures 12.5*a-b*). But the benefits and the mental aspects of the vertical jump are different from those of the standing long jump.

The average high school male athlete with some training should be able to jump up on a 36-inch (91-centimeter) box, and elite athletes should be able to jump up to 56 inches (142 centimeters). When my son Matt was in eighth grade, at 5 feet, 7.5 inches (172 centimeters) and 132 pounds (60 kilograms), he jumped to a 38-inch (97-centimeter) height. Reaching that level made him smile for days. Likewise, you'll hear statements such as, "Wow! I never thought I could do that!" Those benefits alone make box jumping worth the effort.

FIGURE 12.5 It's important to frequently test improvements in jumping ability. The single-leg jump is a good way to test jumping ability, and using an electronic force platform makes it easy and quick *(a-b)*.

It's great to have a lineman who is 6 feet, 4 inches (193 centimeters) tall; weighs 270 pounds (123 kilograms), and can bench-press 450 pounds (204 kilograms) and squat 600 pounds (272 kilograms). But if that same lineman only vertical jumps 24 inches (61 centimeters) and runs 40 yards (37 meters) in 5.0 seconds, something is missing. Plyometrics can increase the vertical jump to 30 inches (76 centimeters) and improve the 40-yard (37-meter) dash to a respectable 4.7 seconds. For the running back who runs 4.6 and has average lateral movement, plyometrics can make the difference between being a good player and being a great one. Plyometric training is definitely worth your time!

CHAPTER 13

Speed Training

During the off-season, athletes should perform speed training on Tuesdays and Thursdays and lift on Mondays, Wednesdays, and Fridays. Speed technique workouts should also be performed twice per week during the in-season.

Athletes should be tested for speed twice per month on either a 40-yard (37-meter) or a 20-yard (18-meter) sprint. They should record their times so that they can chart their progress. Give athletes a trial run at 75 to 90 percent speed and then have them run three timed sprints, recording the best of the three times.

Sprint workouts last about 10 minutes. Five of those minutes should be devoted to technique. Concentrate on only one weakness in form at a time (such as the position of the head, eyes, back, arms, legs, or foot plant) before going on to another. Video analysis is a great way to learn precisely what needs work. Athletes enjoy seeing themselves, and videotape heightens their awareness of proper sprinting technique.

The remaining five minutes of the speed workout should be devoted to doing 10 all-out quality sprints at distances ranging from 10 to 50 yards (9-46 meters). Athletes should have about 30 seconds of rest between sprints so that they are breathing easily before their next sprint.

Of course, you must consider that the Bigger Faster Stronger (BFS) program is designed for a class setting and for sports that require short-term endurance. For example, football players go all out for 2 to 5 seconds and then must be ready for the next play within 10 to 30 seconds.

Angela Williams has one of the best sprint start in the world.

Athletes training for maximum speed need more rest time between sets; one popular method is to rest one minute for every 10 yards (9 meters) of running.

When the weather is bad, do not stop sprinting. Let your competitors take it easy. In Minnesota, waiting for warm weather would mean avoiding sprints for six months. Replace 40-yard (37-meter) sprints outdoors with 20-yard (18-meter) sprints indoors. Times for the two distances will generally differ by about 2 seconds; thus 3.0 seconds for 20 yards (18 meters) is equivalent to 5.0 seconds for 40 yards (37 meters).

TEN WAYS TO IMPROVE SPEED

Carl Lewis ran 9.92 seconds at the Seoul Olympics for a new American record in the 100 meters. Lewis won the gold medal after Ben Johnson tested positive for steroids. Lewis stated that he had run as fast as he could, but this wasn't true. Lewis made four critical errors and probably could have run as fast as 9.87 seconds that day. First, he turned his head three times to look at Johnson—that's three errors. Because he turned his head, Lewis was unable to be as fluid as he could have been. His fourth error was letting up 2 or 3 yards (2-3 meters) before the finish line.

The point of this story is that paying attention to the details is essential to improving your speed, even with elite athletes such as Carl Lewis. With that lesson, here are 10 guaranteed ways to improve your speed:

1. Sprint train twice per week, minimum.
2. Run 10 sprints, varying from 10 to 50 yards (9-46 meters).
3. Time your sprints twice per month (record and chart all times).
4. Sprint all year round. In bad weather, run the 20-yard (18-meter) dash for time indoors.

5. Use video analysis. It can be extremely valuable!
6. Perform flexibility training six times per week (see chapter 14). To improve speed, you must stretch correctly.
7. Perform plyometrics twice per week, minimum.
8. Parallel squat. If you squat but don't go parallel, you will not improve speed maximally. You must squat to parallel, no exceptions!
9. Perform the straight-leg deadlift to strengthen and stretch the glutes and hamstrings at the same time.
10. Practice power cleans to develop an explosive start.

FAST FROM THE START

One of the most important aspects of running fast is getting a good start. Here are the proven ways to get the best start possible, as demonstrated by Kevin Devine, fastest player in the NFL in 1998 and 1999 (see figure 13.2). Kevin, who was with the Jacksonville Jaguars, used the modified BFS track stance at the NFL combine and ran the 40-yard (37-meter) dash in 4.2 seconds.

Learn the modified BFS track stance. No college scout or pro scout makes a note about whether you use a track stance or a football stance. All they do is mark down your time, so you might as well do it right. Here are some valuable tips for getting into the BFS track stance:

- **Hands.** Your thumb and first finger should be on the starting line. Your fingertips should support your weight.
- **Feet.** A rule of thumb is to place one foot 4 to 6 inches (10-15 centimeters) behind the line and the other foot back an additional 12 inches (30 centimeters).
- **Head.** Keep your head down. When it is up, you will tighten up.

Figure 13.1a shows a poor starting position. The hips are high, the back is arched, and the sprinter is looking at the ground. This athlete will be unable to get full power from the legs and will have to take time to adjust his posture and focus to get started—time a sprinter cannot afford to lose.

Now look at figure 13.1b. The back knee is down and the body is relaxed. In this position, you are at "On your mark." Raise your hips higher than your shoulders. Shift your weight as far forward as possible. Your shoulders should be way out in front of your hands. Although this

FIGURE 13.1 Poor starting position with the hips too high (a) and better starting position with the hips lower. Note that the head is still higher than optimal (b).

position is uncomfortable, you'll have great forward momentum for a super start. You are now at "get set." One arm comes way up on "set." On "go!", that arm punches forward with great power and the back leg simultaneously does the same. The left arm and right leg explode forward at the same time. As you begin to sprint, stay low and extend your back leg completely. Keep your arms at a right angle and your arm movement extremely vigorous.

BFS SPRINT TECHNIQUE

Sprinting can be very technical, which is one reason why many sprinters don't hit their peak until they are in their late 20s or even their 30s. But you can master the basics if you follow the BFS sprint technique system. This system consists of the following eight techniques:

1. Your head should be upright.
2. Your eyes should be fixed, looking straight ahead (on target).
3. Your toes should point straight ahead.
4. Your back should be upright and slightly arched.

5. Your shoulders should rotate vigorously, with the elbows fixed at 90-degree angles.
6. Your wrists should simulate a whip action as the shoulders rotate back.
7. Your feet should make the initial plant directly under the hips, not out in front of the body.
8. Your forward leg should initially lift forward, not up. The lower leg should hang before planting with the foot and toes up. Your back knee should extend fully on the follow-through.

FIGURE 13.2 Kevin Devine, formerly the fastest man in the NFL, demonstrates the perfect form for the sprint start.

Those are the basics of BFS speed training. If you follow those simple guidelines and train consistently, you'll be amazed at how fast you can become.

Eden Prairie High School: 28-0!

With 3,100 students, Eden Prairie High School is the largest high school in Minnesota. In 2007 the school was ranked by *Newsweek* in the top 1,200 U.S. high schools, and 71 percent of the school's teachers hold master's degrees or higher. Last year *Sports Illustrated* said Eden Prairie had the best athletic program in the state, and their success has earned the Eagles 26 state championships since 2002. If you're a football player who's fond of winning, you can't find a much better program than the one at Eden Prairie.

Much of the recent success in football for the Eden Prairie Eagles is due to the efforts of Mike Grant, son of former Minnesota Vikings head coach Bud Grant, who led his Vikings to four Super Bowl appearances. The saying, "Like father, like son," definitely applies—Mike Grant has led his teams to six state championships, and they are currently enjoying a 28-0 streak.

Grant, who also serves as athletic director, played football at St. John's University in Minnesota. He had the opportunity to be coached by, and coach with, John Gagliardi, the winningest coach in the history of college football.

> *continued*

> *continued*

State champs!

Grant also has a strong BFS connection; in 1979 and 1981, BFS president Bob Rowbotham was his assistant football coach at Forest Lake High School in Forest Lake, Minnesota. Grant has brought out Rowbotham on several occasions to jump-start the school's program with BFS clinics.

Knowing that Eden Prairie has one of the most successful high school programs in the country, along with some of the best mentors in the sport, we wanted to spend a few minutes with Coach Grant to see what he has learned.

BFS: What do you remember most about John Gagliardi?

Grant: John not only has a brilliant understanding of the fundamentals of the game but also knows how to put the whole program together. He taught me how to make kids believe in your system.

BFS: Were there any special challenges as an athlete, or as a coach, in having such a famous father?

Grant: One of the things that happen when you are the son of a coach is that no one ever thinks that you earned the right to play or coach—they think that you're just handed a starting position or a coaching job.

BFS: Why did you decide to become a football coach?

Grant: Actually, I wanted to become a history teacher first, and I've coached a lot of sports other than football, such as tennis and softball. I would say that I got into coaching because I love being around kids.

BFS: Is there any special emphasis you have in your conditioning program?

Grant: We don't put much emphasis on size, and we're always being outweighed by everybody we play. Our emphasis is on speed and agility and explosive strength, so we focus on the dot drill and plyometrics and the power clean. Our kids really focus on the clean, and in fact we can correlate the success of our teams with their cleans. We know, for example, that if we have a lot of kids cleaning between 240 and 280 pounds (109-127 kilograms), then we are going to have a pretty explosive team.

BFS: What are the major tests you use for your athletes at the beginning of the season?

Grant: The clean, bench press for reps, dot drill, and vertical jump. The vertical jump is a great way to measure explosiveness, and we use the BFS Just Jump pad, so it's really fast—just step up, jump, and give us a number. We don't test on the 40-yard (37 meter) dash because if kids haven't done the squat workouts the way they should, they could have a hamstring issue. Plus, I'm more interested in how quick an athlete is on a 10-yard dash rather than a 40.

BFS: Can we assume that a big bench press doesn't mean that much to you?

Grant: A big bench press doesn't impress me much, but often the kids who can bench-press a ton can do so because they have big chests and short arms. Last year our quarterback, who weighed 215 pounds (98 kilograms), could clean 280 pounds (127 kilograms)—that is an explosive athlete.

BFS: With your success, is there a temptation for kids to only play football?

Grant: Actually, no. My son was a quarterback, and he was also the captain of the basketball team and the captain of the track team. Our starting fullback is the starting third baseman, our starting tailback competed in track, and our all-state left guard is on the basketball team and is a pitcher on the baseball team. In fact, on our baseball team, which was the runner-up in state last year, out of our nine starters, six were football players.

BFS: What value do you see in encouraging kids to play multiple sports?

Grant: Every time you compete in another sport, whatever sport it is, you become a better football player because it teaches you to be able to deal with the stress of playing at a high level. One year we only

> *continued*

> *continued*

> had three kids who had ever played in varsity competition in any sport, and when they went on the field for that first game, they were nervous and lacked confidence.
>
> *BFS:* What type of advice would you give young coaches?
>
> *Grant:* If you're going to be a coach, you've got to be in it for the right reasons. You have to want to coach because you will have great relationships with kids and have fun—we always ask our kids, "If this isn't fun, then why are we doing it?"

CHAPTER 14

BFS 1-2-3-4 Flexibility Program

There are two reasons why the Bigger Faster Stronger (BFS) 1-2-3-4 flexibility program is important to any athlete's training. First, we stretch for speed and jumping power—we've found that athletes often shave two-tenths of a second off their 40-yard (37-meter) dash and increase their vertical jump by 4 inches (10 centimeters). Second, we do each stretch perfectly, using the principles of the six absolutes (see chapter 5).

After giving thousands of BFS clinics over the past three decades, we've found that stretching is the one component most often missing in an athlete's training. This omission is odd considering the tremendous amount of research available on the value of stretching, not just for athletes but also for those who simply want to improve their quality of life. The United States is becoming a nation of couch potatoes, and as a result we have made ourselves far less flexible than ever before. BFS is determined to reverse that trend, and the only way to make that happen for athletes is to incorporate flexibility training into a total program.

BFS regards stretching as a separate exercise regimen alongside regimens such as plyometrics and weight training. Stretching is not part of a warm-up or cool-down for physical activity that athletes only need to do occasionally. They must stretch daily in both the off-season and the in-season. A stretching regimen involves serious work, concentration, and adherence to proper technique.

Just as a coach analyzes every aspect of an athlete's performance, we take stretching seriously and look at every detail. Everything must be perfect. We want athletes to look like sprinters when stretching so that all the limbs and joints are straight and perfect. We use the six absolutes and ask, "Are the knees aligned? Are the toes aligned?" Most coaches don't consider those to be important aspects of stretching. Attention to detail is what makes our program unique and, more important, what makes our program work.

The BFS 1-2-3-4 flexibility program is perfect for everyone, although some people may progress faster than others and achieve different results. In addition, women tend to be more flexible than men, especially on the adductor (inner-thigh) stretch. Athletes should avoid comparing themselves with others and should just focus on self-improvement by making themselves more flexible.

For every athlete who is super tight, another may have too much flexibility. In wrestling, some kids are so flexible that you just can't pin them, no matter how hard you try, because their extreme flexibility allows them to wriggle out of a pin. But they never win because they're so weak. That's the reason we sometimes hear athletes say, "Why do I need to be really flexible? There's Joe, and he's really flexible and he can't jump 10 inches [25 centimeters]—so what's the big deal about flexibility?" The answer is balance.

The goal of stretching is not to set out to become super flexible, but to have muscles that are balanced. We want to make strong athletes more flexible and flexible athletes stronger. When athletes have both flexibility and strength going for them, they have a competitive edge.

Athletes can gain several benefits by following the BFS 1-2-3-4 flexibility program. Here are a few:

- Increased joint range of motion
- Increased speed
- Improved overall performance
- Improved posture
- Decreased number and severity of injuries

The benefits of stretching go beyond injury prevention and rehabilitation. Many movements in athletics require exceptional levels of flexibility that may take years of stretching to develop and daily workouts to maintain. For example, if baseball pitchers can get their arms back a little farther, they will throw harder and faster because they can accelerate the arm over a longer distance. When golfers can get their arms and shoulders back 2 inches (5 centimeters) farther, they can add 20 yards (18 meters) to their drives. Everyone has seen someone who is not particularly strong but has such a huge range-of-motion arch in their golf swing that they can hit the ball 300 yards (274 meters). And if football players can improve flexibility in the hip flexors so that their stride length is 2 inches (5 centimeters) greater, that alone may improve a 40-yard (37-meter) dash time by two-tenths of a second.

The BFS 1-2-3-4 flexibility program is especially useful for increasing running speed. Kevin Devine, who was one of the fastest players in professional football, believes that stretching is key to developing speed. Says Devine, "If you don't stretch hard every day, you will never be as fast as you could be." Although he certainly has a genetic gift for running, Devine says he has made the most of his talents with stretching. "You stretch to win," he says. "It's that simple."

BFS STRETCHING PROGRAM

Our mission at BFS is to provide coaches with a stretching program that will benefit athletes and be feasible in coaching situations where time, facilities, and working with large numbers of athletes are primary considerations. We considered all these factors in developing the most appropriate stretching regimen for BFS.

Although there are several types of stretching, including one called *myofascial release* that stretches the fascial tissue of the body, for practical purposes there are basically two types of stretching: static and dynamic.

Dynamic stretches involve movement and static stretches involve no movement. Proprioceptive neuromuscular facilitation (PNF) is the best type of static stretching, but it requires a partner and takes more time and considerable instruction to perform safely. Ballistic stretching is a type of dynamic stretch where people bounce while they stretch, and if not properly warmed up they have a higher risk of possible injury to the muscle. The BFS power balance drills are dynamic stretches, but in contrast to ballistic stretching, the athlete is in full control of the movement throughout the entire range of motion.

At BFS, we decided that the simplest yet most practical and effective stretching program would be exercises that use the conventional static stretching method, or stretches in which the muscles are passively lengthened and then held in the stretched position for prolonged amounts of time. The advantage of static stretches is that athletes can learn them easily and perform them without a partner. Performed correctly, static stretching produces less muscle tension and offers more safety than other stretching methods. Injuries from static stretching are virtually nonexistent, a claim that cannot be made about other stretching methods.

Although static stretching can be one of the safest types of exercise, athletes should not stretch under certain conditions. For example, stretching the muscles around a recently fractured bone or around an area that has been recently sprained or strained, especially in the back or neck, is usually not a good idea. Here are a few other guidelines:

- **Warm up before you stretch.** Stretching is not a warm-up. To avoid injury, your muscles should be warm before you stretch. The BFS dot drill (see chapter 11) is a perfect warm-up because it will help you break a light sweat.
- **Stretch in the proper environment.** A firm, nonskid mat is ideal for stretching, and the area in which you're stretching should be free of distractions so that you can concentrate.
- **Stretch slowly and gently.** Be forceful when you stretch, but always stretch slowly, moving gradually into each stretch and easing out of every stretch smoothly and slowly.
- **Listen to your pain.** Do not force a joint to the point that you feel pain. You do need to be uncomfortable, but do not extend a joint beyond the point of discomfort. Never yank, pull, or jerk, but do stretch hard. You should be sweating at the end of a stretching workout.
- **Concentrate on breathing.** Proper breathing methods can significantly enhance the quality of your stretching program. Don't hold your breath. You should breathe normally, trying to ease deeper into a stretch during each exhalation.
- **Don't overdo it.** Although this topic is subject to continual debate, you'll gain the greatest benefit from stretching by holding each position for at least 30 seconds. But for beginners, especially those who are extremely tight, performing three sets of 10-second holds is an effective alternative.
- **Personalize your routine.** You should consider your individual needs when designing a stretching program. For example, if you are hypermobile in the knee joint, striving to increase the flexibility of your hamstrings may not be a good idea. If you are an athlete in a sport that requires exceptional flexibility in one area of the body, such as a swimmer who needs flexible shoulders, you may want to add a few extra stretches for that area.
- **Vary your routine.** You should occasionally vary the stretches you perform. We recommend that you experiment with these other stretches only after you have performed the standard BFS 1-2-3-4 flexibility program for several months.

- **Stretch after workouts.** Most coaches and sport therapists agree that the best time to stretch is after a workout, especially when it comes to preventing hamstring pulls. Dr. Michael Ripley is a specialist in flexibility therapy who worked with 10 sprinters who won medals in the Sydney Olympics. Ripley says that after training, muscles often develop a higher level of tension than they had before the training. He says, "This tension will cause muscles to shorten, and without postexercise stretching I've found that over time this causes shortening of the athlete's range of motion. In my opinion it's most important to stretch immediately after the workout because you help keep the body symmetrical. In contrast, if you waited several hours, you'd have to stretch for a considerably longer time to achieve the same effects."

If the training environment is crowded and time is short, such as in a classroom situation, athletes would be better off stretching at home. If facilities are spacious and plenty of time is available, the ideal scenario would be to stretch after performing the dot drill and again at the end of the workout. Stretching in a group environment may also be effective to ensure that this important work gets done.

Static stretching can be performed as a team or individually.

The System

We have created a stretching program that takes about 10 minutes per session and thoroughly stretches every major area of the body, especially the trunk, hips, and legs. The program has been field-tested in thousands of high schools and used by countless athletes of all ages, so we know it works. After athletes learn the program, they can stretch anytime, anywhere, and without a partner.

The BFS stretching program is as easy as 1-2-3-4. Those four numbers help everyone understand and remember the program. Specifically, the program consists of 11 stretches (see figure 14.1), divided into four groups, performed in the following order:

1. On a bench
2. Standing
3. On a wall
4. On the floor

The numbers *1-2-3-4* refer both to the order in which the athlete performs each group of exercises and to the approximate number of minutes the athlete devotes to each group of exercises. Thus, the athlete spends one minute performing stretches while sitting on a bench, two minutes while standing, three minutes in contact with a wall, and at least four minutes while sitting on the floor.

Each stretch should be held for at least 30 seconds, although it's fine to hold a stretch up to 60 seconds to create a higher degree of relaxation. Stretches involving single limbs are performed for 30 seconds on each side for a total of one minute. Beginners have the option of holding each stretch for only 10 seconds, performing three sets per stretch to equal 30 seconds. Now, let's get on to the workout.

One on the Bench (One Stretch for One Minute)

- **Hamstring stretch.** Keep your leg locked and the toes vertical or toward the chest. Pull your upper body forward and spread the chest. Perform for both legs.

Two Standing (Two Stretches for Two Minutes)

- **Latissimus stretch and pectoral stretch.** For the latissimus stretch, cross your hands and raise your arms above your head and as far back as possible. For the pectoral stretch, cross your hands behind your back and raise your arms up and back as far as possible.

Three on the Wall (Three Stretches for Three Minutes)

Perform the following three stretches for three minutes on the wall.

- **Back-leg stretch.** This stretch works the calf muscle called the *gastrocnemius*. Keeping your feet flat on the ground, one foot ahead of the other, and your hands on the wall, move your hips forward. Your back foot and toes should be straight and pointed forward. Perform for both legs.

- **Achilles stretch.** This stretch affects the calf muscle called the *soleus*, which is attached to the Achilles tendon. This stretch is similar to the back-leg stretch except that you keep your knee slightly bent with the heel 1 inch (3 centimeters) off the floor. Squat to increase the intensity of the stretch. Perform for both legs.

- **Quadriceps stretch.** With one hand on the wall, grasp one foot and pull your leg straight up and away from your buttocks. Hold your knee at a 90-degree angle. You should pull the knee straight back, never out to the side. Perform for both legs.

Four on the Floor (Five Stretches for Four or Five Minutes)

Perform the following five stretches over four to five minutes.

- **Abdominal stretch.** Lie flat on the floor. Put your hands on the floor, shoulder width apart (as if you were about to perform a push-up), and straighten your elbows to create an arch in your back. For beginners, just support yourself on bent arms until your flexibility improves. Athletes with any back injuries should check with an appropriate health care professional to determine if this exercise may aggravate their injury.

- **Adductor stretch.** With your feet as far apart as possible, grab your ankles or feet and pull your torso slowly toward the floor. If you can't reach your toes, place your fists on the floor behind you and push forward.

- **Gluteus maximus stretch.** Begin twisting your torso carefully and then press one knee firmly with the opposite arm, forcing your knee to the other side of the lower leg. Switch to the other side.

- **Groin stretch.** Sit with the bottoms of your feet together and grab your ankles. Pull in and press down toward the floor with your elbows on your thighs.

- **Hip flexor stretch.** Place one foot about 24 inches (61 centimeters) in front of the opposite knee. Now place your hands on the bent knee and force your hips forward and down. Spread your chest and keep your eyes straight ahead and your back upright. Do not bend over or put your elbows on your knee—you will be wasting your time. Perform for both legs.

Hamstring

Lat and pec

Back-leg stretch

Achilles

Quads

Abs

Adductor

Glute

Groin

Hip flexor

FIGURE 14.1 The stretches of the BFS flexibility program.

Measuring Progress

As in weight training, measuring progress and setting records in a stretching program will help keep an athlete's motivation high. To measure progress with the BFS 1-2-3-4 flexibility program, we recommend that athletes take the sit-and-reach test at least once a month.

The sit-and-reach test measures flexibility in the back of the legs (hamstrings) and the lower back. To perform the test, sit on the floor with your legs together (putting your legs against a box will help keep your feet from moving). Reach as far as possible and hold for three seconds. Place a yardstick with the 6-inch (15-centimeter) mark at your heels and the 1-inch (2-centimeter) mark closest to your body (see figure 14.2). Reach as far as possible and check results against the BFS standards for the sit-and-reach test (table 14.1).

FIGURE 14.2 Perform the sit-and-reach test once a month a measure your increase in flexibility.

After a few weeks of BFS stretching exercises, you will begin to enjoy significant improvements in flexibility and overall athletic ability. Just 11 minutes of intelligent stretching each day is a painless way to move closer to your goals. Athletic programs at many schools (maybe even your competition) neglect flexibility training. It's a smart move to use the BFS 1-2-3-4 flexibility program to put those critical minutes to work for you.

Table 14.1   BFS Standards for Sit-and-Reach Test

Grade	Males	Females
Excellent	6 in. past heels	8 in. past heels
Good	2 in. past heels	4 in. past heels
Fair	2 in. short of heels	0 in. at heels
Poor	6 in. short of heels	4 in. short of heels

PART IV

Program Administration

CHAPTER 15

Organization and Weight Room Design

We at Bigger Faster Stronger (BFS) believe that you should build your program around six core exercises: the box squat, parallel squat, hex-bar deadlift, power clean, towel bench, and bench press. As such, your first priority is to make certain that your program setup, organization, and equipment allow you to complete all six core lifts in one week. The next step is to look for equipment for auxiliary exercises based on the amount of time, space, and money you have.

According to safety expert Dr. Marc Rabinoff, who has been an expert witness in over 300 legal cases involving sport and physical fitness, an estimated 50 percent of all the litigations involving weight training are a result of poor facility design. One of the major problems is having too much equipment for the space available. Often this is a result of school administrators or gym owners listening to the advice of equipment manufacturers who ignore safety considerations so they can sell as much equipment as possible. Safety is discussed in greater detail in chapter 16, Safety and Liability.

BLUEPRINTS FOR SUCCESS

One valuable service the exercise equipment companies can offer is two-dimensional or three-dimensional weight room illustrations. These illustrations should be drawn to scale to show exactly how a weight room can look, thereby ensuring proper use of available space and the best design for safe traffic flow. For example, the basic minimum standard is at least 2.5 to 3 feet (76-91 centimeters) of space around a piece of equipment. However, more space would be needed for certain pieces of equipment, such as treadmills.

One issue to be careful about when purchasing equipment is to consider the intentions of the person who is using the computer program to design the weight room. People who are selling you equipment may disregard safety standards and simply try to maximize the available space to put as much of their equipment in it as possible.

Regardless of who is consulting with you on the weight room layout, it is your responsibility to make certain there is adequate space for the equipment to be used safely. That may mean checking with the manufacturers, rather than the marketers or distributors, to determine the actual spacing needs and other important installation factors, such as whether or not a piece of equipment must be bolted down to be used safely.

Some weight training machines have a counterbalance system with levers that extend behind them, and there are special precautions that need to be taken for these machines. For example, there should be warning labels on the machine from the manufacturer, such as "Steer clear of moving parts" or "Stand back while in use." In addition, the coach and every athlete using the gym must understand how the machines work.

One way to reduce the risk of injury is to use warning signs. Post warning signs all over the place, not just on the equipment. Also have general weight room rules posted on the walls. For detailed design standards and recommendations for facility design and exercise equipment standards, the bible in this area is the *Annual Book of ASTM Standards*. Founded in 1898, ASTM International is a nonprofit organization that consists of committees working to provide standards for materials, products, systems, and services. In many lawsuits, the ASTM's annual publication provides much of the primary authoritative reference material.

WEIGHT ROOM DESIGN

To ensure a high level of performance and maximum safety in your weight room, follow these commonsense guidelines for designing, upgrading, and maintaining your weight room. Figure 15.1 illustrates what an ideal weight room should look like. Table 15.1 lists equipment suggestions for each of the four core lift stations.

- **Do not use homemade equipment.** The money saved using homemade equipment not designed by reputable manufacturers is not worth the risk of injury.

FIGURE 15.1 The ideal weight room should be large enough to allow many athletes to train at the same time and with enough space to do it safely.

Table 15.1 Equipment for Four Core Stations

Power clean	Squat and box squat	Hex-bar deadlift	Bench and towel bench station
• Lifting platform (or two rubber mats) • 310 lb Olympic set • Set of bumper plates (5, 10, 25, 45 lb) • 15 lb Olympic bar • Two bumper plate racks (one on each side of platform) • Chalk bin • Wrist straps • Two lifting belts (small, medium)	• Squat rack or power rack • 500 lb Olympic set • Three squat boxes (small, medium, large) • Two plate racks (one on each side of rack) • Two lifting belts (small, medium)	• Lifting platform (or two rubber mats) • Hex bar (with the option of a mega-hex bar) • Two plate racks (one on each side of platform) • Two 45 lb bumper plates • 400 lb total in plate weights • Wrist straps • Three lifting belts (small, medium, large)	• Olympic bench • 310 lb Olympic set • Towel bench pad

169

- **Bolt equipment to the floor when possible.** Bolt to the floor all equipment that must be secured to the floor by design.
- **Position weight trees near appropriate racks, benches, and platforms.** Reduce traffic flow and risk of injury from walking with plates by keeping weight trees close to the racks and benches they support.
- **Provide adequate space between equipment.** To ensure that spotters can move freely and do their job, allow at least 48 inches (122 centimeters) between racks and benches, although at least 3 feet (91 centimeters) would be preferable.
- **Ensure all equipment is in good repair.** Replace, repair, or remove all worn or damaged equipment immediately, paying special attention to cables. Post signs on equipment being repaired so that it will not be used.
- **Provide lifting belts.** Keep enough belts on hand for athletes who need them, and supply a variety of belt designs appropriate for the various lifts.
- **Place weights on the bars properly.** The lettering should be on the inside so you can be certain the correct weight is on the bar. Also, placing the weights this way allows for a more secure grip on the plate.
- **Use collars whenever possible.** If there is weight on the bar, use collars on the bar. Keep an adequate supply, plus four extra in case of breakage, so that no athlete is forced to lift without them.
- **Return equipment to appropriate areas.** There should be place for everything and everything in its place! There should be nothing on the floor, such as weight plates or belts, that could cause someone to trip.
- **Maintain proper heating and air conditioning.** Supply appropriate heating, cooling, ventilation, and air conditioning.
- **Have water available.** Provide water coolers or drinking faucets.
- **Have a safety orientation.** Have all students complete a safety curriculum at the beginning of each cycle: Watch videos, read posters, and demonstrate safety spotting techniques. Provide written materials about your safety practices to parents and administrators.
- **Have a first-aid plan.** Keep a first-aid kit and appropriate emergency procedures on hand, as well as forms for documenting injuries.
- **Use posters.** Prominently display posters listing gym rules and safety guidelines.

Organization and Weight Room Design

- **Establish and enforce a dress code.** Do not allow athletes to lift while wearing inappropriate clothing and footwear. Prohibit any jewelry that has the potential to cause injury.
- **Clean vinyl upholstery daily.** Use soapy water or a disinfectant to maintain maximum sanitation.
- **Vacuum and mop at least once a week.** Vacuum to improve sanitation and appearance.
- **Keep a maintenance log.** Monitor your maintenance to ensure compliance.

Do-It-All Stations

The trend in weight room equipment and organization is to have one station do it all for core lifts and some major auxiliaries (figure 15.2). The Ohio University strength and conditioning facility exemplifies this trend.

With 10,000 square feet (929 square meters) and 33 individual do-it-all stations, the Bobcat training facility is one of the most impressive

FIGURE 15.2 An elite half-rack enables athletes to perform all the BFS core lifts, and many auxiliaries, in one area.

weight rooms among Division I universities. Athletes can do benches, inclines, squats, presses, jerks, cleans, and various other lifts at each station. In addition, each station has a chin-up bar and a pair of ab slings. Only bumper plates are used, and the 33 stations include a whopping 17,800 pounds (8,074 kilograms) of plates. By having three athletes per station, a strength coach can train 99 athletes at the same time on the same core lift.

What are the advantages of these stations? Each core lift has a unique time constraint. For example, it takes longer to complete a given number of sets on the parallel squat than it does on the bench press. Therefore, if you have four squat stations and four bench stations with a system of rotating from one to another, you can run into problems. The athletes doing the bench finish their sets before the athletes who are squatting. What do you do? Well, the athletes could stretch, do a burnout set, or do an auxiliary lift, so the situation need not be unproductive or a waste of time. The one-station, do-it-all concept, however, is more efficient.

Coaching is easier because everyone is doing the same lift. Your time management is more precise and controlled. The athletes can be more intense and competitive with everyone doing the same lift. Finally, in most cases, the one-station approach can save space. Figure 15.2 shows examples of single-station units.

Using the Weight Room

A great way to organize a high school or college weight training program is to handle it similar to a practice for a team sport. Here is how:

- **Require the same discipline.** Athletes should be on time and have the feeling that they are participating in a sport practice in the weight room. Athletes should be attentive, hustling, and team oriented. Let your competitors allow their weight training to be a social hour.

- **Instill a team-concept approach.** Make gains as a team and take team pride in individual records. You could have contests between juniors and seniors or between your team and another team. Coaches must be active just as they are in a team practice, constantly motivating and teaching. Let your competitors make workouts dull and lacking in team pride.

- **Organize time and total program efficiently.** Wouldn't it be great if the opposing football coach spent all his practice time on offense and did absolutely nothing with defense or the kicking game? Let your competition work only on weights or concentrate largely on the upper body or bodybuilding. With the BFS total program, you work each important area with just the right amount of time. You work on flexibility and agility every day. You lift three times per week, concentrating on the legs and hips with total-body lifting movements such as the squat and the power clean. You work on speed and plyometric training twice per week in the off-season. You also spend time working on technique skills by position and sport. Set aside some time (five minutes) on Tuesdays and Thursdays to discuss subjects such as nutrition, rest, and strategy. You could also offer a short motivational story once a week.

- **Do some activities outside class.** Does a forward in hockey go on the ice and practice with the goalie? Does a quarterback go out and throw with the receivers on his own? Of course! Why not extend this concept to your training program? Let your competitors stretch for 15 minutes of the 42-minute physical education class. Let your competitors become frustrated and exclaim, "We can't get to it. There isn't enough time!"

- **Give athletes a chance to excel, a chance to reach their potential.** If athletes are truly committed to winning, most of them will stretch and do agility drills outside class time. All a coach has to do is test on Tuesdays and Thursdays to verify the athletes' commitment. Athletes can also do some plyometric, speed, and technique work on their own. Also, having athletes sign commitment contracts or goal cards can help make success happen.

- **Require disciplined spotting and good technique.** A gymnastics coach wouldn't say, "OK, this group is the B squad. Do anything you want." Your competitors might be that way in the weight room, but you should always have spotters who encourage their teammates to give their best. Every athlete should be keenly aware of the coaching techniques of every lift and accept the responsibility of being a coach while spotting.

- **Modify the program intelligently.** One of the workouts in our four-week cycle is to do five sets of five reps, and another is a 5-4-3-2-1 workout. A 42-minute physical education class isn't long enough to do that many sets. Therefore, we recommend doing three sets of five and 5-3-1 for those respective workouts. This modification sacrifices only a small amount of physical development and allows enough time to do it right. Be creative in your use of time and equipment.

- **Don't scrimmage.** All coaches should do some lifting, but there are too many disadvantages to coaches doing their own training during the athletes' workout time. Although athletes respect a coach who keeps in shape, it is just too difficult to teach and motivate properly if coaches are busy lifting. Occasionally, a coach with the required ability might demonstrate factors such as intensity, poundage, and technique.

WEIGHT ROOM ESSENTIALS

Several items are necessary in every weight room. At BFS we recommend lifting belts, lifting straps, knee wraps, and wrist wraps.

Lifting Belts

Lifting belts help protect the spine by increasing intra-abdominal pressure that serves to decompress the spine and by providing feedback on the position of the spine as the athlete lifts. Coaches should have three kinds of belts—the powerlifting belt, the Olympic lifting belt, and the training belt—in a weight room.

- **Powerlifting belt.** The powerlifting belt, also known as a power belt or a squat belt, is a double-notched, 4-inch (10-centimeter) belt used in the sport of powerlifting. This belt is the same width all the way around (see figure 15.3a). Many power belts on the market are twice the thickness of a noncompetitive leather belt. Athletes should use this belt when they squat because it provides frontal support in keeping the body upright and sitting tall, which is hard to do when lifting maximal weights. Athletes should use a power belt in competition and for setting new personal bests, because this is when the athlete requires the most support.

- **Weightlifting belt.** This belt is about the same size as the power belt but tapers around the front of the body in the buckle area (see figure 15.3b). It may not be as thick or as heavy as the power belt (the official size of the Olympic lifting belt for competition is 10 centimeters, which is slightly smaller than 4 inches). This belt is most effective for training and competing in the Olympic lifts, the snatch, and the clean and jerk. The Olympic lifting belt enables the lifter to bend down without the belt digging into the stomach, and it provides sufficient support during the action of the lifts. This belt can also be used effectively in the deadlift because the tapering in the front allows for full bending over. Throwers can use this belt for the hammer, discus, and shot put because of its support and allowance of flexibility.

- **Training belt.** Athletes, lifters, and hobbyists often use a 6-inch (15-centimeter) noncompetitive belt, which is 6 inches wide in the back and tapers down to 2 inches (5 centimeters) in the front. Many feel that the training belt gives the best support for the lower back (figure 15.3c), especially with overhead lifts. Sanctioned powerlifting or Olympic lifting meets don't allow use of this belt, which is for personal training only. If an athlete really likes the feel of it then it is permissible to use it for certain lifts, but for lifts that use heavy weights, the powerlifting and weightlifting belts are a better choice.

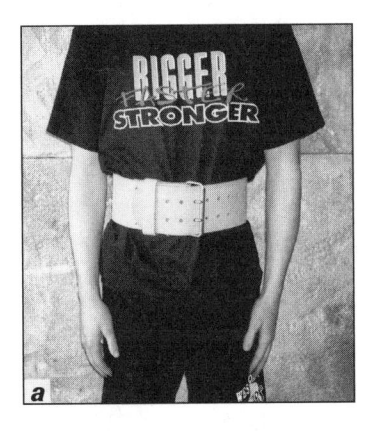

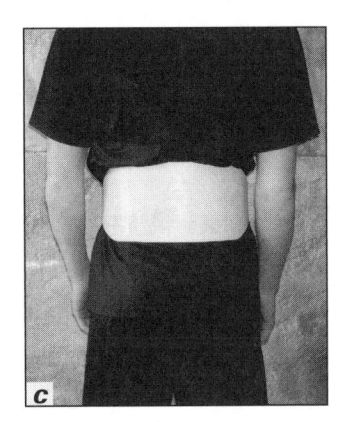

FIGURE 15.3 Powerlifting (a), weightlifting (b), and training (c) belts.

Lifting Straps

Wrist straps can be used in the power clean, the hex-bar deadlift, or any heavy pulling exercises in which the strength of the hands can limit the amount of weight used. These exercises are not designed to develop wrist and hand strength, and therefore it would be a mistake to allow weakness in the hand and wrist to hamper total-body development in these power exercises. The wrist straps help an athlete focus on the acceleration of the bar and prevent slippage and skin abrasions to the palm area. To develop grabbing power, however, some athletes playing certain positions in football might not want to use straps.

Wrist straps should be 1.5 inches (4 centimeters) wide and long enough to wrap once completely around the bar (figure 15.4). Straps made from slick materials are not recommended. Good straps are made from canvas or leather. All straps eventually wear out, so it is important to check frequently for tears that may lead to breakage. Athletes must not lift with worn straps.

Using wrist straps is relatively easy, but you must develop finger dexterity and coordination to use them quickly and efficiently. At first, using straps may seem awkward, but with practice you will quickly get the hang of it. To begin, simply put your hand through the loop. The

FIGURE 15.4 Lifting straps.

end of the strap should be on the same side of the bar as the thumb. Then you are ready to wrap the strap around the bar as tightly as possible. Now grip the rolled-up strap with your fingers and thumb to lock the strap into place. Follow the same procedure with the other hand.

Knee Wraps

Knee wraps (see figure 15.5) should be available to all athletes but should be used sparingly. Some athletes believe that when lifting heavy weights, the wraps encourage good technique by providing feedback on the position of the knees. Knee wraps also may be recommended by doctors for certain injuries, such as tendonitis. Some lifters wrap their knees for every set, but squatting with knee wraps hinders the development of the tendons and ligaments of the knee.

But nearly all powerlifters wear knee wraps in competition. A lifter can squat more weight with knee wraps. Therefore, when athletes are going for heavy sets or new one-rep maxes, knee wraps provide physiological and psychological support. Some athletes will have sore or tender knees, and knee wraps may make squatting easier and more tolerable. Knee wraps also keep the knee joint warm and therefore better lubricated with synovial fluid.

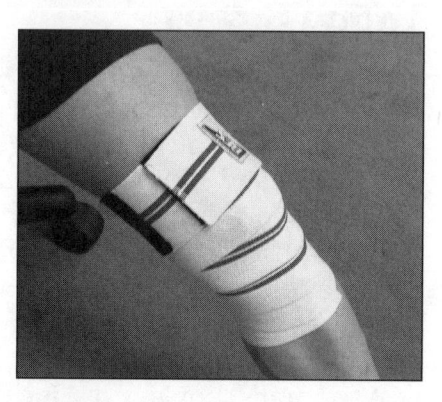

FIGURE 15.5 Knee wraps.

Wrist Wraps

Many athletes get sore wrists from doing power cleans or even bench presses. Incorrect technique and poor flexibility often cause this soreness. When the power clean is done correctly, the bar will rest on the deltoids as the athlete racks it. The wrists should never fully or primarily support the bar.

Wrist wraps (see figure 15.6) are helpful as a training aid for the clean. They give great support to the wrist and might prevent a wrist injury if an athlete has incorrect technique. They feel good and probably give some psychological support. Once you try them, you won't want to lift without them.

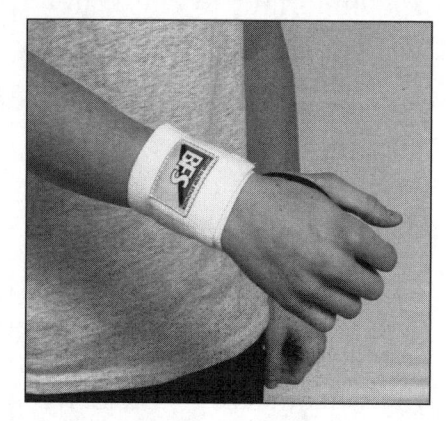

FIGURE 15.6 Wrist wraps.

CHAPTER 16

Safety and Liability

There is a belief that when it comes to the possibility of getting sued, coaches have little to worry about. After all, most coaches are dedicated to helping athletes achieve their physical potential and would never consciously do harm. Everybody understands that coaches should be held in high regard because they are teachers, and as such, isn't it reasonable to expect that their good intentions would be rewarded with a degree of legal immunity? Not quite. The United States has become an increasingly litigious society, and coaches are just as vulnerable as anyone else to becoming involved in a lawsuit.

There is no guaranteed way to avoid lawsuits. You can be sued by anyone, at any time, for just about any reason. That's the way the legal system works. Your aim should be to not give anyone a reason to want to sue you and to put yourself in the best possible position to win a lawsuit. To help you accomplish these two goals, here's some expert advice from Marc Rabinoff.

Dr. Rabinoff is a professor in the Department of Human Performance, Sport, and Leisure Studies at Metropolitan State College of Denver, Colorado. Possessing graduate degrees in administration and physical education, Dr. Rabinoff is one of the most respected sport and fitness liability consultants in the nation. Since 1980, he has served as an expert witness in nearly 300 lawsuits involving coaches, physical educators, schools, health clubs, and equipment manufacturers. He has represented both plaintiffs and defendants, and he has developed valuable insight into identifying the best approaches for his clients. Currently he is a consultant for Bigger Faster Stronger (BFS) who contributes regularly to our magazine and Web site.

In this chapter, we present Dr. Rabinoff's views on many aspects of safety and liability that are a concern to school administrators, coaches, and the parents of athletes.

LAWSUITS: ARE YOU AT RISK?

In the past, lawsuits against coaches certainly happened, but over the past two decades there has been a tremendous increase in the number of lawsuits against equipment manufacturers and weight room operations. Nowadays parents of athletes are not content to just sit back and view coaches as if they couldn't do anything wrong. For example, we're seeing lawsuits that deal with how coaches treat their athletes and even lawsuits involving sexual harassment. Most of the litigations Dr. Rabinoff has worked on commonly relate to duty, standards of care, instructor qualifications, failure to warn and lack of supervision, equipment design deficiencies, and inadequate equipment maintenance.

To learn how the legal system works, it's important to understand the concept of duty. *Duty* refers to the responsibility, or duty, of one person to another for safety. In a lawsuit, the plaintiff (i.e., the person suing) first needs to establish that the defendant had a duty to her at the time of an injury. If there's no duty, there's no lawsuit. After duty is established, the next step is for the plaintiff to show that the duty was breached and that the injury was a result of the defendant's actions. Then the plaintiff must show that the breach actually happened at that facility, a legal concept called *proximate cause*. Finally, the plaintiff must prove that there were damages.

Many strength coaches and personal trainers believe that they are safe from lawsuits because people will go after the organizations they work for, such as schools and health clubs. However, lawyers try to name as many defendants as possible to share fault, following the deep pockets theory. In most states it is the responsibility of the court to determine the balance of the defendants' responsibility to the plaintiff. "In a case I worked on in 1997, $2.3 million was awarded to the plaintiff, with $1 million coming from one insurance carrier, $750,000 from another insurance carrier, and $850,000 from one manufacturer," says Rabinoff.

Can't a health club or school avoid problems simply by hiring independent contractors? The answer is no—the trainee can still sue the health club. Says Rabinoff, "If a health club is saying to the client that their trainers are working in their facility and using their equipment, they support them being here, and when the club is named in a suit, the

Cluttered facilities and improperly maintained equipment increases the risk of accidents and lawsuits.

trainer will be named also. That being said, I strongly recommend that a health club, or any organization involved in physical fitness, have an attorney review their contracts for independent employees as to what their liability is." Regarding waivers, Rabinoff says that they usually don't hold up in a court of law. Instead of a waiver, what a health club wants is assumption-of-risk documents that prove that the person involved in an activity understands the risks involved.

One of the most frequent lawsuits against coaches is in the area of professional instructor qualifications, such as when a gym or health club does not have instructors with recognized academic degrees, certifications, or appropriate courses in continuing education. The idea is that instructors named in lawsuits must provide evidence that what they were doing was professionally correct according to current standards and that the injury was unforeseeable.

In theory, a certification means you went through some course of study, you were tested and evaluated, and you are now certified to perform a particular task. A certification is a document that says you put forth the effort, cost, and time to learn; you want to learn more; and you've achieved a measure of proficiency. But Rabinoff believes that coaches should look beyond earning certifications: "What I recommend for anyone in this field is to get a degree, whether it be an associate degree or a four-year degree in such areas as human performance of sport, physical education, adult fitness, or exercise science. These kinds of programs are offered in colleges and universities throughout every state. It's the longest course of study available to prospective trainers: You take actual college-level classes, you actually do have to perform, and you do learn the basics. After earning a degree, you can then focus on getting certified through groups in particular fields of expertise."

Are certification organizations liable for the actions of those who receive certifications from them? "I get asked that question all the time," Rabinoff says. "I sit on the boards of some of these certification organizations and I say, 'Look, at an entry level, if giving out information is what your certification is for, then go ahead and do it.' However, if you say that this person can actually perform a skill, such as being able to mechanically spot a squat, that's different. A certification may not reflect the person's actual competence unless you've asked the right questions and truly have measured the level of his or her knowledge. So far I haven't seen plaintiff attorneys take on national certification organizations for being inadequate or incompetent in their programs, but I believe that will change. We could start seeing some lawsuits coming back to these organizations because the certifications weren't rigorous enough academically and from a practical perspective did not prove that the persons certified could actually do what they said they could do."

Unfortunately, most of the certifications for personal training, exercise leaders, and strength coaches don't require their graduates to physically perform those skills. In order for you to truly know, for example, how to safely spot a squat, you've got to practice spotting a squat. "If a certification organization says that if you watch this video or read this

Continuing education, such as with coaching certifications, is important to reduce the risk of lawsuits.

textbook you're OK to go out and teach squatting, there's a problem," says Rabinoff. "Think about it: If you knew of a medical school that did everything 'virtual,' would you want to be the first patient of a doctor who had just graduated from there? Would you want to be the first client of someone who had never pleaded a case in court, even though he had graduated from law school and had passed the bar exam, which is a written exam? Would you want someone who had just become a dentist to work on your teeth even if she had the newest, best drill on the market but no one had really made her try it? I wouldn't!"

With many insurance companies, you have to be a member of an organization to purchase the insurance. There are some carriers that offer personal liability insurance to those who are not members of a professional organization, but they are the exception. Usually the criterion to qualify for insurance is being a member of a professional organization, because that validates the fact that at least you're getting professional journals and you may be going to some seminars. Again, it's not enough to have degrees or certifications; you must show that you are keeping current on what is going on in your field. If not, it is often difficult for gyms or health clubs to stand behind the skills and abilities of their instructional staff.

REALITY OF COACHING

We all know that athletes get hurt in sport. Physical educators have to do everything they can to ensure that athletes can move on to a higher level. But you can't have gymnasts perform double twisting backs when they can't even do a forward roll. And just because a freshman is heavy, it doesn't mean he's ready to play on the varsity team, especially if he can't run 20 feet (6 meters) without gasping for air. There's a learning curve, with intermediate steps that must be achieved and documented to show that the athlete was able to perform physically and mentally at that level. Otherwise, you're putting the athlete in jeopardy and the risk of injury skyrockets. One of the most common mistakes coaches make today is that they rush their athletes. Most sports medicine doctors will tell you that 85 percent of the injuries they see are overuse injuries. That's because the trainees' muscles were not ready to do what they were asked to do.

There is the argument that sports with the highest injury rates should be banned, such as gymnastics. But when you do that, the next sport in line moves up and that becomes the high-risk sport. As you keep banning sports, soon all you'll have left is chess! Rabinoff notes that gymnastics is not, as many people believe, the sport with the most injuries, but the injuries found in gymnastics are the most catastrophic ones. "You might only see one injury on a high school gymnastics team in five years, but that injury might be a broken neck," he says. "So it isn't just the number of injuries that scares school administrators, it's the severity of those injuries that causes them to try to cut those sports in their curriculum."

Another issue is allowing athletes with injuries to play. Often football players with minor injuries go back into a game. How should coaches deal with these situations to avoid lawsuits? This is a matter of common sense. There should be checks and balances in athletic programs with a series of people who should have their say on whether an athlete is ready to come back, including athletic trainers, team physicians, the athlete's personal physician, and the coaching staff. All of these people should be involved in determining whether an injured athlete can be allowed to play or practice and at what level.

With the popularity of weight training, often weight rooms become overcrowded with equipment. As mentioned in chapter 15, companies that sell exercise equipment frequently do a free weight room analysis. Using a computer program, they will show how to put their equipment into a facility and lay it out to maximize available space. But if you're going to have weight equipment, you have to make certain there is adequate space, and that may mean checking with the manufacturers, rather than the marketers, to determine what the actual spacing needs are. There are standards in weight room design that should be referenced when designing weight rooms.

For example, the minimum standard is at least 2.5 to 3 feet (76-91 centimeters) of space around a piece of equipment. But that's just for most exercise equipment; with a treadmill Rabinoff believes you should have at least 6 feet (183 centimeters) behind the end of a treadmill and at least 3 feet (91 centimeters) on each side: "What I've seen in cases that I've testified in is the gym owner lines up the treadmills looking out into the workout area, with the end of the treadmills facing a wall with maybe a foot behind them. I've done three cases where people have fallen off the treadmill, hit their head on the wall, and died of trauma! Also, if you don't have enough space between the treadmills, there is the risk that when someone gets on the treadmill and another gets off, they could hit each other." Refer to the previous chapter for specific ideas on how to properly equip and design a weight room.

What is the distributor's responsibility in providing equipment that is safe? At BFS, we believe that if you're putting your name on something, then you should be responsible for what it is. If you're distributing equipment made in Taiwan and they used the wrong kind of bolt so that if users get up to a certain poundage the bolt breaks and causes injury, then the distributor is partly responsible. It's not just a matter of who is making a piece of equipment but also who is selling and marketing it. If you're misrepresenting the equipment you sell, that's fraud, and there are many cases where distributors were sued because they misrepresented what their products could and could not do.

One popular misconception is that machines are safer than free weights. About 95 percent of the litigations Rabinoff has been involved in were related to machines. "My conclusion after 25 years of testifying is that most people know that if you drop free weights you're going to get hurt, so we tend to be really cautious about using them," he says. "With machines, most people think that nothing could happen to them, so they become less safety conscious and tend to use more weight than they should. It seems people have this false sense of security with machines, but the fact is that machines are machines—they have moving parts that can cause injury if you do not use them properly. You have to insert the pins correctly, you have to read the warning signs and follow the instructions, and so on. That's why machine manufacturers are getting better with their instruction plaques and warning statements they put on machines. It may be common sense to most people that you should not try to adjust a machine that is jammed, but to protect themselves, equipment manufacturers and gym owners need to take steps to make certain their clients are aware of such dangers."

BFS is cautious about recommending any new piece of exercise equipment because not every exercise or every method of exercising is good for everyone. When you attach something like an elastic band to a barbell that you are going to bench press, then you have to understand how that band works along with the muscle group that you're working. It's a whole new variable. Likewise, Rabinoff says that coaches should not allow their athletes to use any exercise machine without understanding all its safety operation procedures: "Let's talk about Smith machines, because I just did two cases where the users became quadriplegics. Some people think the process of disengaging the bar and then rotating your hand forward or back to reengage the hook over the pin is the safety mechanism. That's not the safety mechanism! It's the operating mechanism of the apparatus, because you can't do a Smith machine exercise without disengaging and then reengaging the hooks. The safety mechanism is the adjustable stop at the bottom. If you have a Smith machine that doesn't have an adjustable stop, you've got a defective Smith machine because there's no safety mechanism on it."

You can't blame an inanimate object for an injury. If the person who gets hurt didn't know how to use a piece of equipment, you can blame whoever was responsible for letting her use that piece of equipment in the first place. Or you can blame the person performing the exercise because she knew how to do it properly and didn't. And if the equipment was poorly designed, you can blame the manufacturer.

At the high school level, there are more students in weight training classes and fewer teachers. Many schools don't have a lot of money to update equipment, so there is a lot of older equipment that may not have been maintained appropriately. Unfortunately, many coaches simply don't do anything about safety until a kid gets hurt and files a lawsuit. The bottom line is that we can significantly minimize the risk of injuring athletes and getting sued by doing our jobs as coaches, teachers, administrators, and club owners and making sure that each day we open the gym door is a new day with a higher standard of care.

CHAPTER 17

BFS Nutritional Plan

When did it get so difficult to figure out what to have for lunch? Go into any bookstore and you'll see rows and rows of publications promoting the latest diet. There are low-carb diets, high-protein diets, and even high-fat diets. There are diets associated with universities and medical centers and diets endorsed by celebrities. Despite all this attention to proper nutrition, Americans eat more poorly than ever.

Just how bad is the typical American diet? Since 1979, the U.S. government has sponsored a major research project to identify preventable health threats and to establish national goals to reduce these threats. The project is now called Healthy People 2010 and involves 350 national organizations and 270 state agencies. According to this government-sponsored research, only 3 percent of Americans eat at least three servings of vegetables daily, only 28 percent consume two servings of fruit, and 64 percent consume more than 10 percent of their calories from saturated fat. That's pathetic!

Worst of all are the consequences that poor nutrition has had for Americans, especially for young people. Currently 11 percent of children and adolescents are obese. Because obesity is linked to poor overall health and 17 chronic diseases, most children born this year will have shorter life spans than their parents and one out of three will develop diabetes. Further, 40 percent of children aged 5 to 8 show at least one sign of heart disease, which includes high cholesterol, obesity, and high blood pressure.

Exercise, which is vital to good health, has been the focus of Bigger Faster Stronger (BFS) since our company started 32 years ago. Thousands of high schools have used our workout programs and hundreds of schools have won state championships in numerous sports after implementing the BFS program. We have always emphasized good nutrition for our athletes, but now we believe it's time to go further and discuss the pros and cons of supplements. As a result, we are committed to including regular features on nutrition in our magazine and on our Web site.

We see value in supplements, but we believe that no supplement will compensate for a poor diet. Food comes first, and we offer articles from experts in the field of nutrition on how to eat properly. Although many excellent diet programs are available, such as the *Paleo Diet* by Loren Cordain, we do not endorse any single program. Rather, we present the best nutrition programs available and have you choose the program or combination of programs that is best for you.

Now let's talk about supplements. Go to a newsstand and pick up any muscle magazine. Between photos of heavily muscled men and artificially enhanced women in provocative poses, you'll find countless ads for supplements. Following even the basic ideas that the writers and advertisers promote, it's easy to figure out that the average trainee would need to spend several hundred dollars a month on supplements. This just has to stop.

The BFS position on nutrition is that people need to first eat well and then consider a multivitamin and mineral supplement. We recommend such a supplement because, according to a study published in the June 19, 2002, issue of the *Journal of the American Medical Association*, it is difficult to obtain all the essential nutrients from diet alone. Of course, for any medical condition that requires a specific nutrition therapy, BFS recommends consulting a health care practitioner trained in this field.

BFS is the leader in fitness education for young athletes, and with the help of outstanding companies such as Pharmanex, we can help athletes reach their goals in competition and in life. The goals of the Healthy People 2010 project are critical for the health of Americans, and BFS is ready with a plan to help achieve them.

To get you started on improving your eating habits, here is a list of the top 10 nutritional guidelines that summarize the key points in these articles. Following these guidelines will vastly improve health and athletic performance.

1. Eat like a caveman. All your meals should contain at least one vegetable and a protein source. A good general guideline is, if it wasn't growing on the earth 10,000 years ago and you can't kill it with a stick, don't eat it! Foods to eat include seafood, meat, vegetables, nuts and seeds, and fruits, such as the following.

Seafood
Shrimp
Cod
Pollock
Catfish
Scallops
Atlantic salmon
Flounder
Sole
Oysters

Meats
Beef
Chicken
Pork
Turkey

Vegetables
Potatoes
Tomatoes
Onions
Carrots
Celery
Sweet corn
Broccoli
Green cabbage
Cucumbers

Nuts and Seeds
Almonds
Walnuts
Pecans
Hazelnuts
Brazil nuts
Pistachios
Macadamia nuts
Coconut
Sunflower seeds
Pumpkin seeds

Fruits
Bananas
Apples
Watermelon
Oranges
Cantaloupe
Grapes
Grapefruit
Strawberries
Peaches
Pears

2. **Avoid the five lethal foods.** Avoiding soda, French fries, potato chips, donuts, and candy helps reduce the consumption of refined sugar and processed foods. These foods offer little nutritional value and have many undesirable side effects due to their high content of salt, refined sugar, saturated fat, and additives. If you crave sugar, eat fruit.

3. **Favor solid foods over liquid nutrition.** Solid foods have many advantages over liquid nutrition such as many of the high-priced protein drinks found in health-food stores. Solid foods are better sources of fiber, which offers many health benefits such as improved digestion. Solid foods provide a greater variety of nutrients and have a low glycemic level, which helps manage your insulin level.

4. **Stay hydrated.** Whether an athlete is trying to lose fat or gain muscle, it is important to stay well hydrated. A general guideline is that you should drink .6 to .7 ounces (18-21 milliliters) of water per pound (.5 kilogram) of body weight, but rather than trying to follow specific formulas, an excellent way to determine if you are hydrated is to check your urine—it should be clear and odorless.

5. **Consume protein from a variety of sources.** Limiting yourself to just beef, eggs, and chicken as primary sources of protein can lead to food allergies. Consider other protein sources such as shrimp, scallops, turkey, and buffalo. Coach Charles Poliquin, who has performed food allergy tests on athletes, has found that if athletes have developed an allergy to a specific food group, they need to stay away from that protein source for two to six weeks before it can be reintroduced into the diet.

6. **Consult with a medical professional if you are considering going on a diet.** Many diets have severe nutritional deficiencies that can cause health problems. It's always best to consult with a health care professional before experimenting with nutritional programs, especially those that are designed for losing weight, because they can result in nutritional deficiencies.

7. **Consider supplementing your diet with a multivitamin.** The American Medical Association recommends a multivitamin, a nutritional aid to avoid nutrient deficiencies. The reason is because many of the foods consumed today have lower nutritional values, often due to poor soil quality, than foods of the past.

8. **Use only pharmaceutical-grade nutritional aids.** One out of four supplements is tainted with substances that may cause you to fail a drug test. It is a tragedy to see athletes face suspension because they used poorly regulated supplements. Several Olympic-level athletes have been stripped of their medals and suspended from competition due to the use of supplements that were tainted with banned substances.

9. **Consult with a medical professional if you are considering taking high doses of nutritional aids.** High levels of some nutritional aids can cause health problems, especially those that can be stored in fat. It's usually best to stick with the manufacturer's guidelines when taking any supplement unless advised differently by a health care professional.

10. **Get an antioxidant scan.** An antioxidant scan is a quick, noninvasive method that will help determine the quality of your diet and can help you determine the effectiveness of any supplements you may be taking. If your nutritional profile doesn't improve after taking a supplement, then it's likely that the supplement does not contain what

the label says or it is not presented in a form that your body can absorb properly.

FROM THEORY TO PRACTICE

One of the problems we've found in helping athletes eat well is that even when they understand these nutritional guidelines, they still often have no idea about what to eat. One way to resolve this problem is to provide examples of healthy meal plans.

The first step in writing a diet plan is determining what foods are good for you and which ones you will be willing to eat on a regular basis. Then you can start planning your meals to stay on the right track.

Figures 17.1 through 17.4 show four detailed diet plans, ranging from 1,100 to 3,200 calories. They were designed by strength coach Charles Poliquin and his team of doctors at the Poliquin Performance Center, and they have been used by many of his elite athletes.

1,100 Calories

Breakfast: 3 oz. smoked salmon, sliced cucumbers and tomatoes

Lunch: 4 oz. broiled sole or flounder cooked with 1 tsp. butter and sprinkled with Parmesan cheese (or other serving of seafood), 1/2 cup cooked vegetable, mixed green salad with 1 tsp. oil

Dinner: 4 oz. wood-smoked or broiled salmon, 1/2 cup cooked brown rice or vermicelli pasta (Pastariso brand), 1/2 cup tomato sauce with extra oregano, thyme, and garlic, grilled vegetables with 1 tsp. olive oil

Snacks: Your choice of . . . Roasted garlic or almond butter on whole-grain cracker or celery; protein shake with freshly ground flaxseed added; handful of raw almonds, hazelnuts, walnuts, Brazil nuts or pumpkin seeds; fresh green vegetable juice; an organic apple, pear, or grapes; sugar-free yogurt; rice cakes with nut butter; 1 whole-grain muffin with 1 tsp. no-sugar-added jam; guacamole and fat-free chips; fresh or dried organic fruit of any kind; 2 oz. cheese; 2 oz. lean hormone-free meat with mustard; hard-boiled egg

Beverages: Your choice of . . . Green drinks: Green Magma, Kyo-Green, or Green Kamut: 1 tsp. 1-3 times per day in water; or herbal teas: cinnamon, chamomile, or green tea with cinnamon stick

---

FIGURE 17.1 1,100 calorie diet plan.

1,800 Calories

Breakfast: 3 eggs, 3/4 cup oatmeal, I tsp. slivered almonds, I tsp. butter

Lunch: 5 oz. turkey white meat, Dijon mustard, gravy, or other sugar-free sauce or condiment, 2 cups spinach salad with 2 Tbsp. Caesar dressing, handful of cashews

Dinner: 6 oz. almond-crusted broiled red snapper, I cup steamed broccoli, I baked yam, I tsp. butter

Snacks: Your choice of . . . 1/2 small fruit, I oz. cheese, I small handful of nuts; I oz. cheese, 36 calories of crackers, I thin slice avocado; I oz. meat, I slice bread, I tsp. canola mayonnaise; I hard-boiled egg; small handful of grapes and nuts

Beverages: Your choice of . . . Green drinks: Green Magma, Kyo-Green, or Green Kamut: I tsp. 1-3 times per day in water; or herbal teas: cinnamon, chamomile, or green tea with cinnamon stick

FIGURE 17.2 1,800 calorie diet plan.

2,400 Calories

Breakfast: 1-8 oz steak, 1 handful of pecan nuts

Lunch: 2 broiled lamb chops, 1 cup barley with herbs and rice wine vinegar, 8 cooked asparagus spears, spinach salad, 2 tsp. vinaigrette dressing

Dinner: 6 oz. stir-fried fish with 1 cup snow pea pods, onions, bean sprouts, red pepper

Snacks: Your choice of . . . Handful of raw nuts (almonds, Brazil nuts, cashews, hazelnuts, sesame seeds, walnuts); small sugar-free yogurt; raw vegetables; 1 fruit (organic apple, pear, or grapes); air-popped popcorn; fiber bar; hardboiled egg; sugar-free rice cakes with nut butter; roasted garlic or almond butter on celery; protein shake with freshly ground flaxseeds added; 1 whole-grain muffin with 1 tsp. no-sugar-added jam; guacamole and fat-free chips; 2 oz. cheese; 2 oz. lean hormone-free meat

Beverages: Your choice of . . . Green drinks: Green Magma, Kyo-Green, or Green Kamut: 1 tsp. 1-3 times per day in water; or herbal teas: cinnamon, chamomile, or green tea with cinnamon stick

FIGURE 17.3 2,400 calorie diet plan.

> **3,400 Calories**
>
> **Breakfast:** 4-egg omelet with onions, pepper, tomato, mushrooms, 1/2 pink grapefruit, 1 Tbsp. almond butter on spelt bread
>
> **Lunch:** 8 oz. tuna, 1 Tbsp. mayonnaise, 2 avocado slices, onions, 2 pieces whole-grain bread, 4 oz. cole slaw, 1 apple
>
> **Dinner:** 8 oz. roast beef, 1 slice cheese, tomato, onion, lettuce, Dijon mustard, 1 cup brown rice, 1 orange
>
> **Snacks:** Your choice of . . . Handful of raw nuts (almonds, Brazil nuts, cashews, hazelnuts, sesame seeds, walnuts); small sugar-free yogurt; raw vegetables; 1 fruit (organic apple, pear, or grapes); air-popped popcorn; fiber bar; hardboiled egg; sugar-free rice cakes with nut butter; roasted garlic or almond butter on celery; protein shake with freshly ground flaxseeds added; 1 whole-grain muffin with 1 tsp. no-sugar-added jam; guacamole and fat-free chips; 2 oz. cheese; 2 oz. lean hormone-free meat with mustard.
>
> **Beverages:** Your choice of . . . Green drinks: Green Magma, Kyo-Green, or Green Kamut: 1 tsp. 1-3 times per day in water; or herbal teas: cinnamon, chamomile, or green tea with cinnamon stick

FIGURE 17.4 3,400 diet plan.

HOW TO KEEP A FOOD DIARY

The final step is for athletes to begin planning their own meals and keeping a logbook of what they eat. Just the simple act of planning reduces the risk of eating poorly because it provides accountability. The plan doesn't have to be elaborate, and there are many computer programs that will do it automatically. Figure 17.5 shows a simple form for meal planning.

A single diet plan does not work for everyone, and the research available about proper nutrition is overwhelming. For serious athletes who want to learn more about good nutrition theory, two excellent books to start with are *The Paleo Diet* by Loren Cordain and *The Paleo Diet for Athletes* by Loren Cordain and Joe Friel. Don't waste another day—now is the time to begin your personal nutrition program!

Daily Food Planner

Day (circle):   M   Tu   W   Th   F   Sat   Sun

Meal	Foods to Eat/ Quantity	Foods Consumed/ Quantity
Breakfast		
Lunch		
Dinner		
Snacks		

On a scale of 1 to 10, how would you rate your diet today?

FIGURE 17.5   A simple meal planning form.

From *Bigger Faster Stronger* by Greg Shepard, 2009, Champaign, IL: Human Kinetics.

CHAPTER 18

Be an Eleven

Champions are not born but made. Only after a lot of hard work and hard choices does an athlete earn the title of champion. Think about Lance Armstrong overcoming testicular cancer and going on to win the Tour de France seven consecutive times. Think about Muhammad Ali winning the gold medal as a light heavyweight in 1960, upsetting Sonny Liston to win his first world heavyweight championship in 1964, and defeating the seemingly unstoppable George Foreman 10 years later. Those were moments created from endless practice, encouragement, and sacrifice.

Everyone dreams of victory, from the tough running back to the shy teen trying out for the school play. Talent and the desire to succeed are just the beginning. We know that we should follow some sort of path to get what we want, and we know that we will confront obstacles along the way. What we may not know is where the right path begins or how to prepare ourselves for the obstacles. And if we are unprepared, we may lose courage and get lost on the way.

That's where the Be an Eleven program comes in. To help young people fulfill their potential, our program seeks to inspire them to set worthy goals, both athletic and personal, and then help them develop action plans to achieve those goals. Along the way, they learn about the importance of making positive choices, keeping their self-respect, and being team players and role models for others. The Be an Eleven program is simply about being successful in all areas of life.

IT ALL BEGAN WITH A NUMBER

The Be an Eleven program grew out of an activity at our clinics. We would have the athletes perform a box squat to demonstrate how great the intensity can be when teammates support us. We would pick a junior on a team and then put a heavy weight on a barbell and ask the athlete to perform as many reps as possible with his or her teammates cheering the athlete on. The athlete would always do a lot more reps than she could do otherwise.

At first we did these exhibitions primarily with football teams. Many years ago I did one for the late Coach Travis Farrar's team at Springhill High School in Louisiana. When it came time to do the box squat, I picked my athlete, and after several warm-up sets I loaded the barbell to 400 pounds (181 kilograms) and then asked the team, "How many games are there in a football season in Louisiana?" They replied, "14." Then I said, "It's really hard to go 14 games, and this young man here is going to show us how hard it is to go all out for 14 games by doing 14 reps on the box squat with this weight." That number worked fine, and during subsequent exhibitions we would always have the chosen athlete perform 14 reps in the box squat. (By the way, the following year the team went to the state championship.)

The complications began when we started doing clinics for other sports. A high school basketball team may play 26 games in a season, and a baseball team may play 30. So we began to ask, "On a scale of 1 to 10, what kind of effort should we give? What do you want to be known for?" Immediately one of the athletes would say, "Ten!" but inevitably someone else would top it by shouting, "Eleven!" at which we would answer, "Eleven? What a great idea! Let's vote on it. On a scale of 1 to 10, how many want to be known as a team that gives a 10? How about an 11?" And it would always unanimously be 11.

WHO IS AN ELEVEN?

If you are an eleven, you are trustworthy and dependable. Elevens are people you can always count on. Elevens are goal oriented and make success happen. They are morally strong. Elevens pull others up spiritually, mentally, and physically. They are pleasant to be around in every situation and among all groups of people. Elevens are loving and respectful to others, especially their family members. Elevens make every effort to be great students. They are leaders and do the right thing, even if criticized. They follow these three rules for success:

- I am worth my highest goal. I deserve success. I will walk, talk, think, and act like that successful person I want to be.
- I will surround myself with positive people, places, and things. I refuse to associate with any person, place, or thing that creates negativity or mediocrity.
- Nothing, absolutely nothing, will stop me from being an eleven!

Anyone can be an eleven! It is simply a matter of attitude. It is not a matter of talent or intelligence, but a willingness to continually try to raise your personal bar of excellence. Changing your attitude will change your life. You can guarantee yourself success with the right mental attitude. A sign in the Dallas Cowboy weight room states, "It takes no talent to hustle." Those who give it their all every day are elevens.

Almost everyone is an eleven some of the time. However, let's be realistic—no one is an eleven all the time. The goal is to be an eleven more of the time. For some, this goal might seem overwhelming, but there are hundreds of ideas and concepts to help. Everyone can make the big time somewhere.

The Bigger Faster Stronger Be an Eleven program brings many things to your attention that you might not have known or otherwise thought important. Your job will be to evaluate yourself critically in relation to the ideas presented and then choose your personal destiny.

Getting Started

The first thing you need to know in your quest to become an eleven is that everyone, regardless of ability, has been blessed with at least one gift. Your talents make you who you are. It is up to you to recognize them and build on them. Elevens strive to distinguish themselves from the average and look for ways to create their own identity. To accomplish this, you will need to concentrate on things that take effort, that express a positive talent, and that make you stand out from the average.

In standing out from the average, you will hold yourself to the highest possible standards so that you can attain your highest personal destiny. That's not all—your example will inspire and help others to attain their true destiny. How do you set those high standards? You do it by establishing your own value system, learning how to judge what brings the most good into your life and the lives of others. Your value system is personal—you should always have the gift of choice. Similar to a sculptor, an eleven chisels away imperfections through awareness and by making good choices.

Hanging Out With the Right Crowd

The people you associate with, the places you go, and the things you do can either help you or hinder you in accomplishing your dreams. We call these people and things *dream keepers* or *dream stealers*. The more you associate yourself with dream keepers, the easier it will be to accomplish your goals and dreams. The more dream stealers you associate with, the more distractions you will face. This section will help you recognize the dream keepers and dream stealers in your life.

- **People.** There are two kinds of people—those who help keep your dream alive and those who steal your dream. People sometimes alternate between being dream keepers and dream stealers. An eleven strives to be a dream keeper more of the time. A dream stealer is someone who tries to get another person to engage in negative behavior.

    If you have worthy dreams and goals, you must constantly be aware of the dream stealers. For example, a person who says that one drink won't hurt you is a dream stealer. People who are engaged in illegal or gang activities are obvious dream stealers. Those people cannot help you get where you want to go in life. Dream keepers will help you keep your dreams alive and help you achieve your goals.

    If you don't know what you want in life, if you don't know what your values are, and if you set your sights low, you are bound to end up where you don't want to be. One way to help determine your values is to see how you answer questions about them. Here are 10 questions to get you started. There is no right or wrong answer—the purpose is to get you thinking carefully about the decisions you make.

    1. Do you have the right to choose to rob somebody at gunpoint?
    2. Can you rob somebody without legal consequences?
    3. Do you have the right to wear a shirt that says "F— you" in a public place?
    4. How about if "F— you" is spelled out?
    5. How about wearing that shirt in school?
    6. Would you ever park your car in a handicapped space even if you didn't have a permit to park there?
    7. What if there were 10 handicapped spaces that were all empty?
    8. You just finished drinking a can of cola and the nearest garbage can is 100 yards (91 meters) away. What do you do?
    9. Your mom tells you to take out the garbage. What do you do and when do you do it?

10. You are with a group and they are taking drugs. What do you do? What if they are using tobacco and alcohol? What if they are stealing a car or vandalizing property?

- **Places.** We can identify two kinds of places. Some places create a wonderful, positive atmosphere, whereas others create a negative environment. Elevens who are trying to improve themselves and achieve dreams and goals must be able to tell the difference between dream-keeper places and dream-stealer places. Again, you must choose wisely. A party with lots of drinking and drugs is a dream-stealer place. Being alone in a car in a remote place on a date can be a serious dream-stealer place for both guys and girls. Elevens never put themselves in places that could steal their dreams.
- **Things.** Some things help you keep your dream alive, and others can steal your dream. Many things can be either dream keepers or dream stealers. A dream-stealer thing will create a negative situation. For example, the Internet can be a wonderful thing, providing information that will help you achieve your goals, or it can be a negative thing, surrounding you with people with negative attitudes. The Internet can help you keep your dream alive, or it can be a dream stealer. You have to decide which it will be for you.

Vince Helmuth: A Champion Who Cares

Vince Helmuth is what you would call a big man on campus. At Saline High School in Saline, Michigan, Vince weighed 250 pounds (113 kilograms) and could bench press 405 pounds (184 kilograms). He excelled in football, basketball, and track and accepted a full-ride scholarship to the University of Michigan, where he saw playing time as a freshman. Vince might have every reason to be cocky and associate only with the most exclusive school cliques, but he is anything but. That's because the biggest part of this big man on campus is his heart.

Although many high school kids indulge in a lot of self-serving activities, when Vince was in high school he spent much of his free time reading to elementary school children and coaching special-needs kids. "Vince has a temperament and personality to work well with everybody, but especially with special-needs children," says his father, Matt. "At the football games and basketball games, he'll always have special-needs kids and kids he has read to who will be giving him high fives. In fact, the day he verbally committed to Michigan he had to leave early so he could babysit a special-needs kid."

> *continued*

> *continued*

Vince Helmuth enjoys working with special-needs kids in his spare time. Vince is an eleven.

"I love being involved with the Special Olympics," says Vince. "Special Olympians are the happiest group of kids you will ever get to coach. They don't complain; they work hard and are always happy to see me." As for why he reads to little kids, Vince says it was always an exciting event when someone from the outside would come to read to his classes when he was in grade school, and he wanted to share that experience with others.

"Vincent has a tremendous work ethic," says head football coach Mike Glennie, also Saline's strength coach. "I have always told people his motor goes 100 miles per hour [161 kilometers per hour], all the time. He is continually working to improve himself and those around him. He understands the value of a team, giving back to his community, and works to raise people up around him. He is a leader and a wonderful role model. Everyone in our school of over 1,800 knows Vincent, and he is a friend to everyone. Vincent is an eleven!"

All in the Helmuth Family

The Helmuths live in Saline, Michigan, a community of about 10,000 just outside Ann Arbor. Matt Helmuth owns a chemical company, and his wife, Annette, owns and teaches at a Montessori school. Vince's older brother, Chris, graduated from Michigan State and has been playing for the New York Jets since 2002. His older sister, Anna, attended the University of Central Florida on a track scholarship. Vince's younger brother, Gabriel, is in high school and has followed the family tradition of excelling in athletics.

Vince started playing sports at the age of 4, participating in tee ball and soccer, but sports were not pushed upon the Helmuth children. His father says, "We always encouraged our children to play sports, but if they'd felt they wanted to grow up and be piano players we would have encouraged them to be piano players. They just gravitated toward sports."

Vince cites his parents as role models for helping him keep his head on straight, and he has always admired his older brother. "Chris was the first guy I ever knew to play college football, and it was a big deal when he signed to play at Michigan State," he says. His brother tells him that it's a misconception to think that NFL players don't work hard in the off-season. "Every year there are hundreds of new players trying to take your position, so you have to work real hard in the off-season. His advice to me is to keep working hard, and don't listen to what others have to say negatively because some people are going to talk bad about you regardless of how good you are at whatever you do."

In looking for the best person to sum up the primary reason Vince Helmuth was selected as the 2006 BFS Male High School Athlete of the Year, we turned to his mother. Says Annette, "I think Vince has always been the type of child other parents would seek out to have as a friend for their children. I even have people call me and say, 'Vince is such a wonderful child.' You know, you never really know how you're doing as a parent until someone else tells you how they are behaving away from you. So I guess we have been doing something right here with Vince."

CHAPTER 19

Why Steroids Don't Work

Athletic glory, monetary riches, and admiration by the public are among the prizes for athletes who excel at the highest levels. On a smaller scale, athletes enjoy a rush of pride and self-respect when they best their opponents. Winning is great, and steroids offer the promise to make athletes winners. And given the number of athletes who have tried these illegal substances, the benefits of steroid use must outweigh the risks, right? Wrong! The truth is that the world's best athletes have proved repeatedly that they don't have to take steroids to achieve the highest level of performance.

Most coaches would say that the statement "Steroids don't work" is absurd. Of course steroids work in the short term, but what about the long term? Do they really give athletes an advantage in a college or professional career? Is it possible for an athlete to perform better without steroids?

Many experts in the field of strength and conditioning define steroids as performance-enhancing drugs. We define them as performance-debilitating drugs. Athletes in mainstream high school or collegiate sports can achieve better results through hard, consistent, and smart training. And professional athletes can have longer, more successful careers by not taking steroids. Following are 11 reasons why steroids do not work in the long run.

Robin Jennings is the president of BFS Baseball. He has never used steroids and was able to play professionally for 12 years with Cincinnati, Chicago, Colorado, and Oakland.

1. Bodybuilders and powerlifters are not the same as athletes from other sports. Bodybuilders don't run, jump, or score goals. Training programs for mainstream athletes and bodybuilders are as different as night and day. Steroids are often purchased illegally through bodybuilders at gyms. Do steroids work for bodybuilders? Sure they do, and that's the problem. An unsuspecting athlete may go to a gym and take advice from a bodybuilder who just stands and flexes. Why would you do that? It doesn't make sense.

2. Steroids are a roller-coaster ride. At first, most people get a great high and a rush of quick strength when they take steroids. This happens because of the increased testosterone intake. Let's say a teenage baseball player is 6 feet, 1 inch (185 centimeters) tall; weighs 190 pounds (86 kilograms); and has a bench press max of 250 pounds (113 kilograms). This teen decides to take some steroids, just one three-week dosage. In four weeks, he has gained 25 pounds (11 kilograms) of weight and benched 290 pounds (132 kilograms). He's on fire! You can't tell him steroids don't work.

This teen had heard about steroids and their dangers, but he thought he would just take one cycle and stop. Certainly that couldn't hurt, and he would get some fast gains. However, by the sixth week, he has lost 10

(5 kilograms) of those 25 pounds (11 kilograms) and his bench is now 275 pounds (125 kilograms). The teen is depressed, so he decides to take another dose. He gets another jolt of strength and weight, but this time it is not as dramatic. His bodybuilding friend advises him to get more sophisticated by changing to a variety of steroids and increasing dosages. Later in the year, our teen joins his college baseball team as a walk-on. He is scared he might get tested so he quits the juice for a while. He tells the strength coach he can bench 350 pounds (159 kilograms), but when he maxes out for him, he can do only 315 pounds (143 kilograms).

Steroids are like any other drug: The user can become a loser. In this case, are steroids working for this teen as a baseball player? How about as a student? As a person?

3. Great gains can be made with intelligence, intensity, and persistence. The Bigger Faster Stronger program has been well thought out and extensively tested. Any young athlete can break eight or more personal records every week, week after week, month after month. There are no ups and downs. Consistent improvement in speed, agility, and jumping records can be made. There is absolutely no reason to take steroids; giant gains can be made without them. Unfortunately, many people do not believe this.

A great strength coach can create a positive intensity. When athletes are surrounded by teammates in the school weight room who have a common goal, they can make greater gains than by working alone in a gym, even with a personal trainer. Same thing happens on the practice field or during the game: Teammates can create an incredibly intense atmosphere.

4. Uncontrolled aggressiveness is bad! Steroids affect hormone levels that control aggression. Many athletes on steroids enjoy physical confrontations. But, you might say, isn't aggression good in sport? This holds true only up to a point. An athlete must have a controlled psyche. When athletes are out of control, they make mistakes or can get thrown out of a game. This obviously contributes to losing, not winning. A football player has a lot to think about to be successful during any play. On offense it starts with correct alignment and the snap count. On defense it starts with recognizing the formation and certain tendencies. A softball player with uncontrolled aggressiveness will strike out because hitting requires a high degree of concentration and skill.

5. Fast workout recovery can be made by intelligent variation and selection of exercises. One big selling point of steroids is their supposed ability to allow a longer, harder workout and a faster recovery time for the next day's workout. The BFS program easily shoots down that advantage. First of all, bodybuilders work out much longer in the weight room than athletes do. It is also common for bodybuilders to lift weights six days a week, alternating upper body one day, lower body the next. Athletes, on the other hand, need only three days a week in the weight room in the off-season and only two days a week during the season. Doing more work than this may cut into time that should be spent working on sport-specific skills. Further, working out too much in the weight room will cause excessive fatigue that can interfere with sport practices. Weight workouts are much shorter: three to four hours per week in the off-season.

6. The possibility of getting caught is stressful. Most users hide their steroid abuse. They will go miles from their home to get their steroids and needles. If they get caught, they could get into serious trouble. Sneaking around and hiding is an obstacle to winning, and it is a detriment to athletes attaining their full potential.

7. Steroids don't help agility, flexibility, or technique. Training to reach athletic potential is complex. Steroid users often place too much importance on size and strength and forget about many other areas that are necessary in winning. Athletes who take steroids and think that greater speed and jumping ability will automatically happen are sadly mistaken. Working on the techniques and skills of the sport is vital. Improvements take time and energy, and athletes who take steroids often minimize the importance of honing their talents.

8. Steroids are a crutch. If athletes look to steroids to help them get through a crucial situation, they have lost the battle. When it's the bottom of the ninth with two outs and the athlete at the plate has the feeling of "Where's my pill?", then the user becomes a loser. During critical times, a winner creates her own intensity and confidence. A winner does not look for external help but looks inside for that something extra.

9. The stronger an athlete gets, the less important extra strength becomes—this is the diminishing return theory. For example, it is not as important to add 100 pounds (45 kilograms) on a bench press that is already at 400 pounds (181 kilograms) as it would be to add the same amount on a 300-pound (136-kilogram) bench. The same concept goes for adding 100 pounds (45 kilograms) to a 200-pound (91-kilogram) bench. This same reasoning would apply to any other core lift, such as a parallel squat and a power clean. Is a Division I college offensive lineman who benches 550 pounds (250 kilograms) going to be better than another lineman who can bench only 450 pounds (204 kilograms)? The answer is no! The same thing is true of a thrower or a power hitter in baseball. It is ridiculous to believe that Jose Canseco could hit more home runs by having a 500-pound (227-kilogram) bench press compared with a 400-pound (181-kilogram) bench press.

There is definitely a point of diminishing returns and even a point of no return in mainstream sport. If you have a 19-inch (48-centimeter) arm and you are a serious bodybuilder, you want a 21-inch (53-centimeter) arm. Get that, and you want a 23-inch (58-centimeter) arm. You want to keep getting bigger and bigger as long as you have high definition. Look closely at the photo of Gregg Valentino. His arms are 27 inches (69 centimeters). The point of no return does not exist for this bodybuilder. When the point of no return does not exist, steroids do.

The massive arm of bodybuilder Gregg Valentino shows that in this sport you can never be too big.

10. Steroid use can cause tendon and ligament injuries. This information has been around for years. If a known steroid user experiences a tendon or ligament injury, steroids are considered a likely cause. Evidence suggests that well-trained nonsteroid users have fewer injuries than steroid users.

Baseball offers some interesting statistics: Trips to the disabled list increased 32 percent between 1992 and the present. In 2001, shoulder injuries almost doubled. Jose Canseco missed more than 600 games from 1989 to the end of his career. That staggering number averages out to missing one ball game for every two appearances. Did steroids cause some of those missed games and injuries? Dr. Charles Yesalis says that it would be wrong to claim that this increase is due to anabolic steroids because we don't know what percentage of people have used them. Some players, coaches, and other experts are not as conservative as Dr. Yesalis and are certain that steroids caused all these injuries. But as shown by the success of Cal Ripken, who never missed a game, it is possible to have a long, healthy career without injuries if you train smart.

11. The best don't do steroids! The vast majority of athletes in mainstream sport don't use steroids. The very best players have proven consistently that they don't need illegal drugs to achieve the highest levels of performance.

Now is the time for every pro, college, and high school athlete to stand with the legendary players of the past and take pride in their hard-won strength and conditioning. Today's players will learn that steroids don't work—that they are the exact opposite of performance enhancing. The legendary players of the future will reach their prestigious levels without steroids.

APPENDIX

AUXILIARY LIFT CHART

Lift	Lift	Lift	Lift	Lift
Sets & Reps	Sets & Reps	Sets & Reps	Sets & Reps	Sets & Reps
Date	Date	Date	Date	Date
Weight	Weight	Weight	Weight	Weight
Sets & Reps	Sets & Reps	Sets & Reps	Sets & Reps	Sets & Reps
Date	Date	Date	Date	Date
Weight	Weight	Weight	Weight	Weight
Sets & Reps	Sets & Reps	Sets & Reps	Sets & Reps	Sets & Reps
Date	Date	Date	Date	Date
Weight	Weight	Weight	Weight	Weight
Sets & Reps	Sets & Reps	Sets & Reps	Sets & Reps	Sets & Reps
Date	Date	Date	Date	Date
Weight	Weight	Weight	Weight	Weight
Sets & Reps	Sets & Reps	Sets & Reps	Sets & Reps	Sets & Reps
Date	Date	Date	Date	Date
Weight	Weight	Weight	Weight	Weight
Sets & Reps	Sets & Reps	Sets & Reps	Sets & Reps	Sets & Reps
Date	Date	Date	Date	Date
Weight	Weight	Weight	Weight	Weight
Sets & Reps	Sets & Reps	Sets & Reps	Sets & Reps	Sets & Reps
Date	Date	Date	Date	Date
Weight	Weight	Weight	Weight	Weight

Only record your major auxiliary lifts, write them in the space at the top then write in the sets, reps, weight and date. Then update this entire page as your weight, time, distance etc. improves. Here are even more Auxiliary and Performance records for you to break. You do not need to record Leg Curls, Leg Extensions, Straight Leg Deadlifts or the Glute Ham Developer.

Vertical Jump		Standing Long Jump		Sit & Reach		BFS Dot Drill		20 Yard Speed		40 Yard Speed	
Date	Height	Date	Length	Date	Inches	Date	Time	Date	Time	Date	Time
Date	Height	Date	Length	Date	Inches	Date	Time	Date	Time	Date	Time
Date	Height	Date	Length	Date	Inches	Date	Time	Date	Time	Date	Time
Date	Height	Date	Length	Date	Inches	Date	Time	Date	Time	Date	Time
Date	Height	Date	Length	Date	Inches	Date	Time	Date	Time	Date	Time
Date	Height	Date	Length	Date	Inches	Date	Time	Date	Time	Date	Time
Date	Height	Date	Length	Date	Inches	Date	Time	Date	Time	Date	Time
Date	Height	Date	Length	Date	Inches	Date	Time	Date	Time	Date	Time
Date	Height	Date	Length	Date	Inches	Date	Time	Date	Time	Date	Time

BIGGER FASTER STRONGER

BFS

SET RECORDS

BOX SQUAT OR SQUAT VARIATION

WEEK 1 3 x 3

3		DATE
3		BODY WEIGHT
3+		EXTRA REPS
		SET TOTAL
3		DATE
3		BODY WEIGHT
3+		EXTRA REPS
		SET TOTAL
3		DATE
3		BODY WEIGHT
3+		EXTRA REPS
		SET TOTAL
3		DATE
3		BODY WEIGHT
3+		EXTRA REPS
		SET TOTAL
3		DATE
3		BODY WEIGHT
3+		EXTRA REPS
		SET TOTAL
3		DATE
3		BODY WEIGHT
3+		EXTRA REPS
		SET TOTAL
3		DATE
3		BODY WEIGHT
3+		EXTRA REPS
		SET TOTAL
3		DATE
3		BODY WEIGHT
3+		EXTRA REPS
		SET TOTAL
3		DATE
3		BODY WEIGHT
3+		EXTRA REPS
		SET TOTAL
3		DATE
3		BODY WEIGHT
3+		EXTRA REPS
		SET TOTAL

WEEK 2 5 x 5

5		DATE	5		DATE
5			5		
5		BODY WEIGHT	5		BODY WEIGHT
5		EXTRA REPS	5		EXTRA REPS
5+			5+		
		SET TOTAL			SET TOTAL
5		DATE	5		DATE
5			5		
5		BODY WEIGHT	5		BODY WEIGHT
5		EXTRA REPS	5		EXTRA REPS
5+			5+		
		SET TOTAL			SET TOTAL
5		DATE	5		DATE
5			5		
5		BODY WEIGHT	5		BODY WEIGHT
5		EXTRA REPS	5		EXTRA REPS
5+			5+		
		SET TOTAL			SET TOTAL
5		DATE	5		DATE
5			5		
5		BODY WEIGHT	5		BODY WEIGHT
5		EXTRA REPS	5		EXTRA REPS
5+			5+		
		SET TOTAL			SET TOTAL
5		DATE	5		DATE
5			5		
5		BODY WEIGHT	5		BODY WEIGHT
5		EXTRA REPS	5		EXTRA REPS
5+			5+		
		SET TOTAL			SET TOTAL

WEEK 3 5-4-3-2-1

5		DATE	5		DATE
4			4		
3		BODY WEIGHT	3		BODY WEIGHT
2		EXTRA REPS	2		EXTRA REPS
1+			1+		
		SET TOTAL			SET TOTAL
5		DATE	5		DATE
4			4		
3		BODY WEIGHT	3		BODY WEIGHT
2		EXTRA REPS	2		EXTRA REPS
1+			1+		
		SET TOTAL			SET TOTAL
5		DATE	5		DATE
4			4		
3		BODY WEIGHT	3		BODY WEIGHT
2		EXTRA REPS	2		EXTRA REPS
1+			1+		
		SET TOTAL			SET TOTAL
5		DATE	5		DATE
4			4		
3		BODY WEIGHT	3		BODY WEIGHT
2		EXTRA REPS	2		EXTRA REPS
1+			1+		
		SET TOTAL			SET TOTAL
5		DATE	5		DATE
4			4		
3		BODY WEIGHT	3		BODY WEIGHT
2		EXTRA REPS	2		EXTRA REPS
1+			1+		
		SET TOTAL			SET TOTAL

WEEK 4 10-8-6

10		DATE
8		BODY WEIGHT
6+		EXTRA REPS
		SET TOTAL
10		DATE
8		BODY WEIGHT
6+		EXTRA REPS
		SET TOTAL
10		DATE
8		BODY WEIGHT
6+		EXTRA REPS
		SET TOTAL
10		DATE
8		BODY WEIGHT
6+		EXTRA REPS
		SET TOTAL
10		DATE
8		BODY WEIGHT
6+		EXTRA REPS
		SET TOTAL
10		DATE
8		BODY WEIGHT
6+		EXTRA REPS
		SET TOTAL
10		DATE
8		BODY WEIGHT
6+		EXTRA REPS
		SET TOTAL
10		DATE
8		BODY WEIGHT
6+		EXTRA REPS
		SET TOTAL
10		DATE
8		BODY WEIGHT
6+		EXTRA REPS
		SET TOTAL
10		DATE
8		BODY WEIGHT
6+		EXTRA REPS
		SET TOTAL

BOX SQUAT OR SQUAT VARIATION REP RECORDS

REP	Establish Records	1st Break	2nd Break	3rd Break	4th Break	5th Break	6th Break	7th Break	8th Break	9th Break	10th Break	11th Break	12th Break	13th Break	14th Break
1	Date / Weight	Date / Weight	Date / Weight	Date / Weight	Date / Weight	Date / Weight	Date / Weight	Date / Weight	Date / Weight	Date / Weight	Date / Weight	Date / Weight	Date / Weight	Date / Weight	Date / Weight
2	Date / Weight	Date / Weight	Date / Weight	Date / Weight	Date / Weight	Date / Weight	Date / Weight	Date / Weight	Date / Weight	Date / Weight	Date / Weight	Date / Weight	Date / Weight	Date / Weight	Date / Weight
3	Date / Weight	Date / Weight	Date / Weight	Date / Weight	Date / Weight	Date / Weight	Date / Weight	Date / Weight	Date / Weight	Date / Weight	Date / Weight	Date / Weight	Date / Weight	Date / Weight	Date / Weight
4	Date / Weight	Date / Weight	Date / Weight	Date / Weight	Date / Weight	Date / Weight	Date / Weight	Date / Weight	Date / Weight	Date / Weight	Date / Weight	Date / Weight	Date / Weight	Date / Weight	Date / Weight
5	Date / Weight	Date / Weight	Date / Weight	Date / Weight	Date / Weight	Date / Weight	Date / Weight	Date / Weight	Date / Weight	Date / Weight	Date / Weight	Date / Weight	Date / Weight	Date / Weight	Date / Weight
6	Date / Weight	Date / Weight	Date / Weight	Date / Weight	Date / Weight	Date / Weight	Date / Weight	Date / Weight	Date / Weight	Date / Weight	Date / Weight	Date / Weight	Date / Weight	Date / Weight	Date / Weight
8	Date / Weight	Date / Weight	Date / Weight	Date / Weight	Date / Weight	Date / Weight	Date / Weight	Date / Weight	Date / Weight	Date / Weight	Date / Weight	Date / Weight	Date / Weight	Date / Weight	Date / Weight
10	Date / Weight	Date / Weight	Date / Weight	Date / Weight	Date / Weight	Date / Weight	Date / Weight	Date / Weight	Date / Weight	Date / Weight	Date / Weight	Date / Weight	Date / Weight	Date / Weight	Date / Weight

SET RECORDS
TOWEL BENCH OR BENCH VARIATION

WEEK 1 — 3 x 3
WEEK 2 — 5 x 5
WEEK 3 — 5-4-3-2-1
WEEK 4 — 10-8-6

TOWEL BENCH OR BENCH VARIATION REP RECORDS

REP	Establish Records	1st Break	2nd Break	3rd Break	4th Break	5th Break	6th Break	7th Break	8th Break	9th Break	10th Break	11th Break	12th Break	13th Break	14th Break
1	Date / Weight	Date / Weight	Date / Weight	Date / Weight	Date / Weight	Date / Weight	Date / Weight	Date / Weight	Date / Weight	Date / Weight	Date / Weight	Date / Weight	Date / Weight	Date / Weight	Date / Weight
2	Date / Weight	Date / Weight	Date / Weight	Date / Weight	Date / Weight	Date / Weight	Date / Weight	Date / Weight	Date / Weight	Date / Weight	Date / Weight	Date / Weight	Date / Weight	Date / Weight	Date / Weight
3	Date / Weight	Date / Weight	Date / Weight	Date / Weight	Date / Weight	Date / Weight	Date / Weight	Date / Weight	Date / Weight	Date / Weight	Date / Weight	Date / Weight	Date / Weight	Date / Weight	Date / Weight
4	Date / Weight	Date / Weight	Date / Weight	Date / Weight	Date / Weight	Date / Weight	Date / Weight	Date / Weight	Date / Weight	Date / Weight	Date / Weight	Date / Weight	Date / Weight	Date / Weight	Date / Weight
5	Date / Weight	Date / Weight	Date / Weight	Date / Weight	Date / Weight	Date / Weight	Date / Weight	Date / Weight	Date / Weight	Date / Weight	Date / Weight	Date / Weight	Date / Weight	Date / Weight	Date / Weight
6	Date / Weight	Date / Weight	Date / Weight	Date / Weight	Date / Weight	Date / Weight	Date / Weight	Date / Weight	Date / Weight	Date / Weight	Date / Weight	Date / Weight	Date / Weight	Date / Weight	Date / Weight
8	Date / Weight	Date / Weight	Date / Weight	Date / Weight	Date / Weight	Date / Weight	Date / Weight	Date / Weight	Date / Weight	Date / Weight	Date / Weight	Date / Weight	Date / Weight	Date / Weight	Date / Weight
10	Date / Weight	Date / Weight	Date / Weight	Date / Weight	Date / Weight	Date / Weight	Date / Weight	Date / Weight	Date / Weight	Date / Weight	Date / Weight	Date / Weight	Date / Weight	Date / Weight	Date / Weight

SET RECORDS
POWER CLEAN

WEEK 1 — 3 x 3
WEEK 2 — 5 x 5
WEEK 3 — 5-4-3-2-1
WEEK 4 — 4-4-2

THE POWER CLEAN REP RECORDS

REP	Establish Records	1st Break	2nd Break	3rd Break	4th Break	5th Break	6th Break	7th Break	8th Break	9th Break	10th Break	11th Break	12th Break	13th Break	14th Break
1	Date / Weight	Date / Weight	Date / Weight	Date / Weight	Date / Weight	Date / Weight	Date / Weight	Date / Weight	Date / Weight	Date / Weight	Date / Weight	Date / Weight	Date / Weight	Date / Weight	Date / Weight
2	Date / Weight	Date / Weight	Date / Weight	Date / Weight	Date / Weight	Date / Weight	Date / Weight	Date / Weight	Date / Weight	Date / Weight	Date / Weight	Date / Weight	Date / Weight	Date / Weight	Date / Weight
3	Date / Weight	Date / Weight	Date / Weight	Date / Weight	Date / Weight	Date / Weight	Date / Weight	Date / Weight	Date / Weight	Date / Weight	Date / Weight	Date / Weight	Date / Weight	Date / Weight	Date / Weight
4	Date / Weight	Date / Weight	Date / Weight	Date / Weight	Date / Weight	Date / Weight	Date / Weight	Date / Weight	Date / Weight	Date / Weight	Date / Weight	Date / Weight	Date / Weight	Date / Weight	Date / Weight
5	Date / Weight	Date / Weight	Date / Weight	Date / Weight	Date / Weight	Date / Weight	Date / Weight	Date / Weight	Date / Weight	Date / Weight	Date / Weight	Date / Weight	Date / Weight	Date / Weight	Date / Weight

SET RECORDS
HEX BAR OR DEAD LIFT

WEEK 1 — 3 x 3

WEEK 2 — 5 x 5

WEEK 3 — 5-4-3-2-1

WEEK 4 — 4-4-2

THE HEX BAR DEADLIFT REP RECORDS

REP	Establish Records	1st Break	2nd Break	3rd Break	4th Break	5th Break	6th Break	7th Break	8th Break	9th Break	10th Break	11th Break	12th Break	13th Break	14th Break
1	Date / Weight	Date / Weight	Date / Weight	Date / Weight	Date / Weight	Date / Weight	Date / Weight	Date / Weight	Date / Weight	Date / Weight	Date / Weight	Date / Weight	Date / Weight	Date / Weight	Date / Weight
2	Date / Weight	Date / Weight	Date / Weight	Date / Weight	Date / Weight	Date / Weight	Date / Weight	Date / Weight	Date / Weight	Date / Weight	Date / Weight	Date / Weight	Date / Weight	Date / Weight	Date / Weight
3	Date / Weight	Date / Weight	Date / Weight	Date / Weight	Date / Weight	Date / Weight	Date / Weight	Date / Weight	Date / Weight	Date / Weight	Date / Weight	Date / Weight	Date / Weight	Date / Weight	Date / Weight
4	Date / Weight	Date / Weight	Date / Weight	Date / Weight	Date / Weight	Date / Weight	Date / Weight	Date / Weight	Date / Weight	Date / Weight	Date / Weight	Date / Weight	Date / Weight	Date / Weight	Date / Weight
5	Date / Weight	Date / Weight	Date / Weight	Date / Weight	Date / Weight	Date / Weight	Date / Weight	Date / Weight	Date / Weight	Date / Weight	Date / Weight	Date / Weight	Date / Weight	Date / Weight	Date / Weight

SET RECORDS
SQUAT

SQUAT REP RECORDS

REP	Establish Records	1st Break	2nd Break	3rd Break	4th Break	5th Break	6th Break	7th Break	8th Break	9th Break	10th Break	11th Break	12th Break	13th Break	14th Break
1	Date Weight	Date Weight	Date Weight	Date Weight	Date Weight	Date Weight	Date Weight	Date Weight	Date Weight	Date Weight	Date Weight	Date Weight	Date Weight	Date Weight	Date Weight
2	Date Weight	Date Weight	Date Weight	Date Weight	Date Weight	Date Weight	Date Weight	Date Weight	Date Weight	Date Weight	Date Weight	Date Weight	Date Weight	Date Weight	Date Weight
3	Date Weight	Date Weight	Date Weight	Date Weight	Date Weight	Date Weight	Date Weight	Date Weight	Date Weight	Date Weight	Date Weight	Date Weight	Date Weight	Date Weight	Date Weight
4	Date Weight	Date Weight	Date Weight	Date Weight	Date Weight	Date Weight	Date Weight	Date Weight	Date Weight	Date Weight	Date Weight	Date Weight	Date Weight	Date Weight	Date Weight
5	Date Weight	Date Weight	Date Weight	Date Weight	Date Weight	Date Weight	Date Weight	Date Weight	Date Weight	Date Weight	Date Weight	Date Weight	Date Weight	Date Weight	Date Weight
6	Date Weight	Date Weight	Date Weight	Date Weight	Date Weight	Date Weight	Date Weight	Date Weight	Date Weight	Date Weight	Date Weight	Date Weight	Date Weight	Date Weight	Date Weight
8	Date Weight	Date Weight	Date Weight	Date Weight	Date Weight	Date Weight	Date Weight	Date Weight	Date Weight	Date Weight	Date Weight	Date Weight	Date Weight	Date Weight	Date Weight
10	Date Weight	Date Weight	Date Weight	Date Weight	Date Weight	Date Weight	Date Weight	Date Weight	Date Weight	Date Weight	Date Weight	Date Weight	Date Weight	Date Weight	Date Weight

SET RECORDS

BENCH

WEEK 1 — 3 x 3

WEEK 2 — 5 x 5

WEEK 3 — 5-4-3-2-1

WEEK 4 — 10-8-6

218

BENCH REP RECORDS

REP	Establish Records	1st Break	2nd Break	3rd Break	4th Break	5th Break	6th Break	7th Break	8th Break	9th Break	10th Break	11th Break	12th Break	13th Break	14th Break
1	Date / Weight	Date / Weight	Date / Weight	Date / Weight	Date / Weight	Date / Weight	Date / Weight	Date / Weight	Date / Weight	Date / Weight	Date / Weight	Date / Weight	Date / Weight	Date / Weight	Date / Weight
2	Date / Weight	Date / Weight	Date / Weight	Date / Weight	Date / Weight	Date / Weight	Date / Weight	Date / Weight	Date / Weight	Date / Weight	Date / Weight	Date / Weight	Date / Weight	Date / Weight	Date / Weight
3	Date / Weight	Date / Weight	Date / Weight	Date / Weight	Date / Weight	Date / Weight	Date / Weight	Date / Weight	Date / Weight	Date / Weight	Date / Weight	Date / Weight	Date / Weight	Date / Weight	Date / Weight
4	Date / Weight	Date / Weight	Date / Weight	Date / Weight	Date / Weight	Date / Weight	Date / Weight	Date / Weight	Date / Weight	Date / Weight	Date / Weight	Date / Weight	Date / Weight	Date / Weight	Date / Weight
5	Date / Weight	Date / Weight	Date / Weight	Date / Weight	Date / Weight	Date / Weight	Date / Weight	Date / Weight	Date / Weight	Date / Weight	Date / Weight	Date / Weight	Date / Weight	Date / Weight	Date / Weight
6	Date / Weight	Date / Weight	Date / Weight	Date / Weight	Date / Weight	Date / Weight	Date / Weight	Date / Weight	Date / Weight	Date / Weight	Date / Weight	Date / Weight	Date / Weight	Date / Weight	Date / Weight
8	Date / Weight	Date / Weight	Date / Weight	Date / Weight	Date / Weight	Date / Weight	Date / Weight	Date / Weight	Date / Weight	Date / Weight	Date / Weight	Date / Weight	Date / Weight	Date / Weight	Date / Weight
10	Date / Weight	Date / Weight	Date / Weight	Date / Weight	Date / Weight	Date / Weight	Date / Weight	Date / Weight	Date / Weight	Date / Weight	Date / Weight	Date / Weight	Date / Weight	Date / Weight	Date / Weight

GOAL RECORD CHART

To use the goal setting chart properly, follow these instructions. <u>Do not record any goals until you have gone through the entire program for 3 to 4 weeks.</u> After this amount of time, you will know exactly what your real starting performance is in all the events. The next step is to decide what you want to achieve in each event at the end of the year, record these figures under "year end goal". You then will set goals one month at a time accomplishing these monthly goals until you achieve your year end goals. Remember to record what you actually achieve after each month to help you to stay on track. Good Luck and remember the "Sky's the Limit."

EXERCISE	MONTH 1	MONTH 2	MONTH 3	MONTH 4	MONTH 5	MONTH 6	MONTH 7	MONTH 8	MONTH 9	MONTH 10	MONTH 11	YEAR END GOAL
BENCH	GOAL / ACTUAL	GOAL / ACTUAL	GOAL / ACTUAL	GOAL / ACTUAL	GOAL / ACTUAL	GOAL / ACTUAL	GOAL / ACTUAL	GOAL / ACTUAL	GOAL / ACTUAL	GOAL / ACTUAL	GOAL / ACTUAL	GOAL / ACTUAL
SQUAT	GOAL / ACTUAL	GOAL / ACTUAL	GOAL / ACTUAL	GOAL / ACTUAL	GOAL / ACTUAL	GOAL / ACTUAL	GOAL / ACTUAL	GOAL / ACTUAL	GOAL / ACTUAL	GOAL / ACTUAL	GOAL / ACTUAL	GOAL / ACTUAL
CLEAN	GOAL / ACTUAL	GOAL / ACTUAL	GOAL / ACTUAL	GOAL / ACTUAL	GOAL / ACTUAL	GOAL / ACTUAL	GOAL / ACTUAL	GOAL / ACTUAL	GOAL / ACTUAL	GOAL / ACTUAL	GOAL / ACTUAL	GOAL / ACTUAL
HEX BAR DEAD LIFT	GOAL / ACTUAL	GOAL / ACTUAL	GOAL / ACTUAL	GOAL / ACTUAL	GOAL / ACTUAL	GOAL / ACTUAL	GOAL / ACTUAL	GOAL / ACTUAL	GOAL / ACTUAL	GOAL / ACTUAL	GOAL / ACTUAL	GOAL / ACTUAL
DEAD LIFT	GOAL / ACTUAL	GOAL / ACTUAL	GOAL / ACTUAL	GOAL / ACTUAL	GOAL / ACTUAL	GOAL / ACTUAL	GOAL / ACTUAL	GOAL / ACTUAL	GOAL / ACTUAL	GOAL / ACTUAL	GOAL / ACTUAL	GOAL / ACTUAL
40 YARD DASH	GOAL / ACTUAL	GOAL / ACTUAL	GOAL / ACTUAL	GOAL / ACTUAL	GOAL / ACTUAL	GOAL / ACTUAL	GOAL / ACTUAL	GOAL / ACTUAL	GOAL / ACTUAL	GOAL / ACTUAL	GOAL / ACTUAL	GOAL / ACTUAL
20 YARD DASH	GOAL / ACTUAL	GOAL / ACTUAL	GOAL / ACTUAL	GOAL / ACTUAL	GOAL / ACTUAL	GOAL / ACTUAL	GOAL / ACTUAL	GOAL / ACTUAL	GOAL / ACTUAL	GOAL / ACTUAL	GOAL / ACTUAL	GOAL / ACTUAL
DOT DRILL (AGILITY EVENT)	GOAL / ACTUAL	GOAL / ACTUAL	GOAL / ACTUAL	GOAL / ACTUAL	GOAL / ACTUAL	GOAL / ACTUAL	GOAL / ACTUAL	GOAL / ACTUAL	GOAL / ACTUAL	GOAL / ACTUAL	GOAL / ACTUAL	GOAL / ACTUAL
STANDING LONG JUMP	GOAL / ACTUAL	GOAL / ACTUAL	GOAL / ACTUAL	GOAL / ACTUAL	GOAL / ACTUAL	GOAL / ACTUAL	GOAL / ACTUAL	GOAL / ACTUAL	GOAL / ACTUAL	GOAL / ACTUAL	GOAL / ACTUAL	GOAL / ACTUAL
VERTICAL JUMP	GOAL / ACTUAL	GOAL / ACTUAL	GOAL / ACTUAL	GOAL / ACTUAL	GOAL / ACTUAL	GOAL / ACTUAL	GOAL / ACTUAL	GOAL / ACTUAL	GOAL / ACTUAL	GOAL / ACTUAL	GOAL / ACTUAL	GOAL / ACTUAL

INDEX

Note: The italicized *f* and *t* following page numbers refer to figures and tables, respectively.

A
abdominal stretch 161, 162*f*
absolutes for perfect technique
   align the knees 60-61, 61*f*
   align the toes 57-59, 58*f*, 59*f*
   athletic or jump stance 51-53, 52*f*
   be tall 53-54, 54*f*
   eyes on target 50, 50*f*
   list 49
   spread the chest 54-57, 55*f*, 57*f*
Achilles stretch 161, 162*f*
adductor stretch 161, 162*f*
aggressiveness, steroids and 203
agility training
   dot drill 133-136, 134*f*, 136*f*, 136*t*
   readiness program 39
   steroids and 204
Aitken, Erin 99-101
alignment. *See* absolutes for perfect technique
align the knees absolute 60-61, 61*f*
align the toes absolute 57-59, 58*f*, 59*f*
all-American chain 112. *See also* lifting chains
Allosso, Kiley 129-130
all-state chain 112. *See also* lifting chains
Annual Book of ASTM Standards 168
ASTM International 168
athletic stance 51-53, 52*f*
attitude, of elevens 195
auxiliary lifts. *See* sport-specific auxiliary lifts
awards, readiness graduation 46

B
back-leg stretch 59*f*, 161, 162*f*
balance drills 126-128, 127*f*, 128*f*
ballistic stretching 157. *See also* flexibility training
bar positioning, for squats 69

baseball
   batting stance 55*f*
   Robin Jennings on 30-33
Be an Eleven program
   beginnings 194
   character traits 194
   dream keepers, stealers 196-197
   objectives 193
   rules for success 194-195
   talents and standards 195
Beat the Computer 7-8
bench press. *See also* towel bench press
   equipment 169*t*
   injury risk 104, 108
   judging criteria 43
   prelift technique 105-106, 105*f*, 106*f*
   problem solving 108
   record-keeping forms 218-219
   spotting 108
   standards 103
   technique 106-108
   in training cycle 19
   variations 108-111, 109*f*, 110*f*, 111*f*, 118, 118*f*
bench press shoulder 104
be tall absolute 53-54, 54*f*
BFS program
   BFS High School Athletes of the Year 90, 129-130, 197-199
   BFS High School of the Year 8-9
   origins vii-xi
   popularity vii
   success stories ix-x, 90-92, 99-101, 137-138, 151-154
bodybuilders, steroids and 202
bodybuilding stance 51
bone density, in young athletes 36-37
bounding drills, plyometric 143, 143*f*
Bounding to the Top (Costello) 140

box jumping, plyometric 141-142, 141*f*, 142*f*
box squat
   equipment 169*t*
   judging criteria 43
   record-keeping
      examples 18*f*
      forms 208-209
   spotting 75, 76*f*
   technique 74-76, 76*f*
   in training cycles 17, 26-27
Brigham Young University ix
burnout set, defined 20

C
certifications, lawsuits and 180-181
champions 193
chest-spreading absolute 54-57, 55*f*, 57*f*
Churchville-Chili Senior High School 90-92
Cole, Jon viii
college programs 6-7
combo hex bar 93, 94*f*
confidence
   Robin Jennings on 31-32
   weight training and 38
Cordain, Loren 191
core lifts. *See* bench press; hex-bar deadlift; parallel squat; power clean
Costello, Frank 140
Cross, Tom 127

D
deadlift. *See* hex-bar deadlift, spotting, deadlift; straight-leg deadlift
Deer Park High School 137-138
Devine, Kevin 149, 151*f*, 157
Dick, Paul 90-92
diets 188. *See also* nutrition
dips 115, 115*f*
dot drill
   benefits 133
   described 134-135, 134*f*, 136*f*
   standards 136*t*
dream keepers, stealers 196-197
duty (legal concept) 178
dynamic stretches 157. *See also* flexibility training

E
Eaton, Mark 28, 83
Eden Prairie High School 151-154

elementary school athletes
   BFS benefits 5-6
   readiness program 40-41
epiphyseal (growth) plate damage 36
equipment and accessories
   core stations 169*t*
   do-it-all stations 171-172, 171*f*
   E-Z Squat 77
   Front Squat Harness 77
   hex bars 93, 94*f*, 95, 97
   hip sled 79-80, 79*f*, 80*f*
   injuries and lawsuit risk 182-183
   knee wraps 176, 176*f*
   lifting belts 174, 175*f*
   lifting chains 80, 80*f*, 111-112, 111*f*
   lifting straps 78, 78*f*, 175-176, 175*f*
   Olympic barbells 7
   parallel squat 67-68
   readiness program 44-45
   safety and liability and 167-168, 182-184
   weight room design and 168-171
   wrist wraps 176, 176*f*
eyes on target absolute 50, 50*f*
E-Z Squat 77

F
Facts and Fallacies of Fitness (Siff) 36
female athletes
   bench press standards 103
   BFS Female High School Athlete of the Year 129-130
   deadlift standards 99
   Lady Flames 99-101
   readiness program 35-38, 45, 45*t*
   squat standards 66
   squat technique 60, 61*f*, 65, 73
Fernholm, Stefan vii, x-xi, 140
flexibility training
   benefits 155-157
   guidelines 158-159, 159*f*
   1-2-3-4 system 160-161, 162*f*
   readiness program 39, 40
   standards 163*t*
   static versus dynamic stretches 157
   steroids and 204
   testing 163, 163*f*, 163*t*
   toe alignment 58-59, 59*f*
food allergies 188
food diaries 191, 192*f*
food supplements 186, 188
Frenn, George vii-viii, 75

Index

Friel, Joe 191
front squat 76-79, 77*f*, 78*f*
Front Squat Harness 77

G
Gagliardi, John 152, 153
GAS 12-13, 12*f*
gastrocnemius stretch 161, 162*f*
general adaptation syndrome (GAS) 12-13, 12*f*
glute-ham raise 115, 115*f*
gluteus maximus stretch 161, 162*f*
goals
    Be an Eleven program 193
    goal record chart 220
    Robin Jennings on 33
Goss, Kim 82
graduation, readiness program 39, 45-46, 45*t*
Granger High School ix
Grant, Mike 151-154
Griffin, Andy 12
grip technique
    bench press 106, 106*f*
    squats 68, 68*f*
groin stretch 161, 162*f*
growth plate damage 36

H
hamstring stretch 160, 162*f*
hand positioning. *See* grip technique
Harvey-Bowen, David 90
Hayashi, Mel 37
Healthy People 2010 185
Helmuth, Vince 197-199
hex-bar deadlift
    benefits 93
    concerns 94-95
    equipment 93, 94*f*, 95, 97, 169*t*
    prelift technique 95
    record-keeping forms 214-215
    versus regular deadlift 94
    standards 98-99
    technique 96-97, 96*f*
    in training cycle 19
    variations 97-99, 97*f*, 98*f*
high-bar bodybuilding squat 80
high hex bar 97
high school athletes
    BFS benefits 5
    BFS High School Athletes of the Year 90, 129-130, 197-199

BFS High School of the Year 8-9
BFS success stories ix, 90-92, 99-101, 137-138, 151-154
    readiness program 38
hip flexor stretch 59*f*, 161, 162*f*
hips, in squats 74
hip sled 79-80, 79*f*, 80*f*
Hoch, John 7-8
hydration 188

I
incline bench press 110-111, 110*f*, 118, 118*f*
injuries
    bench press and 104, 108
    Erin Aitken on 100-101
    lawsuit risk and 182-184
    leg exercises for 120-121, 120*f*, 121*f*
    power clean and 83
    readiness program and 38
    Robin Jennings on 31
    squats and 64-65
    steroids and 205
    young athletes' risk 37
in-season training
    components 26-27
    progress in 28-29, 29*f*
    speed training in 147
    week by week cycle 27
Internet 197

J
Jennings, Robin 30-33
Jordan, Michael 32
jumps
    plyometric program 140-144, 141*f*, 142*f*, 143*f*
    record-keeping form 207
    testing 144-145, 145*f*
jump stance 51-53, 52*f*

K
Klein, Karl K. 64
knees, in squats 60-61, 61*f*, 64-65, 73-74
knees-aligned absolute 60-61, 61*f*
knee wraps 176, 176*f*

L
Lady Flames 99-101
latissimus stretch 160, 162*f*
lat pull-down 118-119, 119*f*

lawsuit risks
    coaches' qualifications and 180-181
    injuries and 182-184
    legal concepts 178
    liable parties 178-180
    weight room design and 167
leg curl 119-120, 119f
leg extension 120, 120f
leg press 120-121, 121f
Lewis, Carl 148
lifting belts 174, 175f
lifting chains 80, 80f, 111-112, 111f
lifting straps 78, 78f, 175-176, 175f
Logansport High School 8-9
logbooks 7
lunges 121-122, 121f

M
marble test 66
meal plans 189, 189f, 190f, 191f. *See also* nutrition
mega hex bar 93, 94f
middle school athletes
    readiness program 38-40
    strength training concerns 35-38
military press 122, 123f
motivation strategies 13
multisport athletes
    periodization and 14-15
    problems for 3-4
    Robin Jennings on 32
multivitamins 186, 188
myofascial release 157

N
neck exercise 122, 122f
nutrition
    food diaries 191, 192f
    guidelines 186-189
    meal plan examples 189, 189f, 190f, 191f
    poor 185
    supplements 186, 188

O
obesity 185
off-season training. *See also* rotational set-rep system
    overview 16, 16t
    speed training in 147
    week by week cycle 17-23
Olympic barbells 7
Olympic-style squat 80

P
Paleo Diet, The (Cordain) 191
Paleo Diet for Athletes, The (Cordain, Friel) 191
parallel squat
    benefits 63, 65
    depth 63, 65-67, 70-71
    equipment 67-68, 77-78, 78f, 169t
    judging criteria 43-44
    knees and 64-65, 73-74
    presquat technique 67-70, 68f
    problem-solving 73-74
    record-keeping forms 216-217
    spotting 71-73, 72f
    standards 66
    technique 60-61, 61f, 70-71, 71f
    in training cycle 19
    variations 79-80, 80f
parents, in readiness program 38
peaking 14
pectoral stretch 160, 162f
penalties 22, 22t
periodization, versus BFS 14-15
personal records
    breaking 11-12, 20, 23
    establishing 18, 18f, 23
Pettyjohn, Barry 137-138
plateaus, overcoming 12-13
plyometrics
    benefits 140, 145
    defined 139-140
    program phases 140-144, 141f, 142f, 143f
    readiness program 39-40
    testing 143, 144-145, 145f
Poliquin, Charles 189
posture 53-54, 54f
poundage
    periodization and 15
    in readiness program 39, 42
power balance drills 126-128, 127f, 128f
power clean
    benefits 82-84
    concerns 81-84
    equipment 169t
    judging criteria 44
    prelift technique 84-85, 85f
    record-keeping forms 212-213
    safety guidelines 84
    spotting 87
    technique 85-86, 86f
    in training cycle 19
    variation 87-89, 89f, 124, 125f

powerlifting
   squats 66-67
   stance 51-52
powerlifting belt 174, 175f
power line 93
power snatch
   benefits 87-88, 124
   described 87
   prelift technique 88
   technique 88-89, 89f, 125f
preparatory plyometrics 139-140. *See also* plyometrics
protein 188
proximate cause 178
push jerk 124, 124f
push press 126, 126f

Q

quadriceps stretch 161, 162f

R

Rabinoff, Marc 167, 177-178
racking, unracking weights 69-70, 71
readiness program
   candidates 35-38
   elementary school 40-41
   equipment 44-45
   graduation 39, 45-46, 45t
   middle school 38-40
   record keeping 42, 42f
   results 41
   strength training details 39, 41-45
record breaking 11-12, 20, 23
record keeping
   auxiliary lift chart 207
   goal record chart 220
   readiness program 42, 42f
   rotational set-rep system
      examples 18, 18f, 19f
      forms 208-219
      importance 17
   spotted deadlift 98
   test results form 207
   unification management 7-8
recovery rates, steroids and 203-204
rotational set-rep system
   adjustments 22
   advantages 11-12
   penalties 22, 22t
   versus periodization 14-15
   record breaking 20, 23
   record keeping
      examples 18, 18f, 19f
      forms 208-219
      importance 17
   Selye's GAS model in 12-13, 12f
   in training cycles 16-21, 16t, 28
   warm-ups 21-22, 21t
rotator cuff tendonitis 104

S

safety. *See also* lawsuit risks
   equipment use and 183-184
   power clean guidelines 84
   weight room design and 167-171, 182-183
School of Height 37
Science and Practice of Strength Training (Zatsiorsky) 37
Sehome High School ix
Selye, Hans 12-13
set-rep system. *See* rotational set-rep system
Shillington, Mark 37
shoulder press 122, 123f
Siff, Mel 36
single-station weight units 171-172, 171f
sit-and-reach test 163, 163f, 163t
software, record-keeping 7-8
soleus stretch 161, 162f
speed training
   readiness program 39-40
   speed improvement 148-149
   sprint technique 41, 58, 58f, 149-151, 150f, 151f
   testing 147
   in training cycles 147
sports fans 32
sport-specific auxiliary lifts. *See also specific exercises*
   advanced lifts 124
   list 116-117t
   objectives 113
   record-keeping form 207
   standard lifts 114
   weekly lifting schedule 114t
spotting
   bench press 108
   box squat 75, 76f
   deadlift 98-99, 98f
   parallel squat 71-73, 72f
   power clean 87
spread the chest absolute 54-57, 55f, 57f
sprint technique. *See also* speed training
   BFS technique 149-151, 150f, 151f
   readiness program 39-40, 41
   toe alignment 58, 58f

squat balance test 73
squat belt 176, 176*f*
squats. *See* box squat; front squat; parallel squat
stance 51-53, 52*f*
standing box jump 143, 144-145, 145*f*
standing long jump 140
standing-tall absolute 53-54, 54*f*
static stretches 157. *See also* flexibility training
steroids
   defined 201
   Robin Jennings on 31
   why they don't work 202-206
Stone, Michael 64-65
straight-leg deadlift
   judging criteria 44
   technique 97, 97*f*, 123, 123*f*
   in training cycle 27
strength training. *See also specific exercises*
   readiness program 39, 41-45
   young athlete concerns 35-38
stress theory 12-13, 12*f*
stretching. *See* flexibility training
supplements 186, 188

T
team training 14
technique. *See also specific exercises*
   readiness program
      judging criteria 43-44
      poundage and 39, 42
   six absolutes
      align the knees 60-61, 61*f*
      align the toes 57-59, 58*f*, 59*f*
      athletic or jump stance 51-53, 52*f*
      be tall 53-54, 54*f*
      eyes on target 50, 50*f*
      list 49
      spread the chest 54-57, 55*f*, 57*f*
testing
   flexibility training 163, 163*f*, 163*t*
   jumps 144-145, 145*f*
   plyometrics 143, 144-145, 145*f*
   record-keeping form 207
   speed training 147
toes-aligned absolute 57-59, 58*f*, 59*f*
towel bench press
   equipment 169*t*
   judging criteria 43
   record-keeping
      examples 18*f*
      forms 210-211

   technique 109, 109*f*
   in training cycles 17, 27
track stance 149-150, 150*f*
training belt 174, 175*f*
training cycles. *See* in-season training; off-season training

U
unification
   benefits 3-4
   college programs 6-7
   defined 3
   elementary, high school programs 5-6
   management 7-8
Utah Jazz ix-x

V
VanDeZande, Roger 7
varsity chain 112. *See also* lifting chains
vertical jump 140
video analysis 147

W
warm-ups
   dot drill 133-136, 134*f*, 136*f*, 136*t*
   rotational set-rep system 21-22, 21*t*
warning signs 168
weightlifting belt 174, 175*f*
weight room
   accessories 174-176, 175*f*, 176*f*
   design guidelines 168-171
   equipment 169*t*, 171-172, 171*f*
   ideal 169*f*
   safety 167-168, 182-184
   use guidelines 172-173
   warning signs 168
weight training. *See* strength training
wrist straps 175-176, 175*f*
wrist wraps 176, 176*f*

Y
young athletes
   BFS benefits 4-5
   hex-bar deadlift 94
   readiness program 38-41
   strength training concerns 35-38
youth hex bar 93, 94*f*

Z
Zatsiorsky, Vladimir 37

ABOUT THE AUTHOR

Greg Shepard is the owner and founder of Bigger Faster Stronger (BFS), which has been providing strength training programs to high schools and colleges for over 30 years. He has coached football at three Division I schools and was a strength and conditioning consultant for the Utah Jazz. He has given more than 500 seminars to coaches and athletes in all 50 states, and more than 9,000 high schools have implemented his BFS program. Shepard is the author of numerous publications, including the *BFS* print magazine, which has a circulation of over 500,000 and is distributed to every high school, college, and professional team in the country.

Shepard earned his doctorate in physical education from Brigham Young University. He is the author of four books and 23 videos on sport conditioning. Shepard is married with four children and lives in Provo, Utah.

You'll find other outstanding sports conditioning resources at

www.HumanKinetics.com/sportsconditioning

In the U.S. call 1-800-747-4457

Australia 08 8372 0999 • Canada 1-800-465-7301
Europe +44 (0) 113 255 5665 • New Zealand 0800 222 062

HUMAN KINETICS
The Premier Publisher for Sports & Fitness
P.O. Box 5076 • Champaign, IL 61825-5076 USA

eBook
available at
HumanKinetics.com